MARCO

Tips

TURKEY
SOUTH COAST

Black Sea
BULGARIA
Istanbul
Ankara
TURKEY
Izmir
GREECE   South Coast
Antalya
SYRIA
Crete   Cyprus
LEBANON
Mediterranean
Sea
ISRAEL
EGYPT

SYMBOLS

INSIDER TIP   Insider Tip

★   Highlight

●●●●   Best of ...

↘   Scenic view

(*) Telephone numbers that are not toll-free

PRICE CATEGORIES HOTELS

Expensive	over 170 lira
Moderate	120–170 lira
Budget	under 120 lira

Prices are for two people in a double room with breakfast, per night

PRICE CATEGORIES RESTAURANTS

Expensive	over 60 lira
Moderate	25–60 lira
Budget	under 25 lira

Prices are for a meal with a starter, main course, dessert and one drink

On the cover: Picturesque alleyways around the harbour p. 52 | Underwater attractions p. 63

CONTENTS

The Turkish Riviera → p. 70

The South East → p. 80

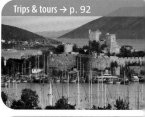
Trips & tours → p. 92

Road atlas → p. 122

MAPS IN THE GUIDEBOOK
(124 A1) Page numbers
and coordinates refer to
the road atlas
(0) Site/address located off
the map. Coordinates are
also given for places that are
not marked on the road atlas

Maps of Alanya, Antalya
Fethiye, Marmaris and Side
can be found inside the
back cover

INSIDE BACK COVER:
PULL-OUT MAP →

PULL-OUT MAP
(A–B 2–3) Refers to the
removable pull-out map

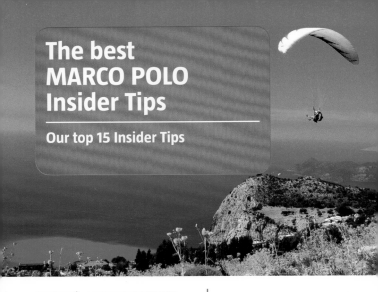

The best MARCO POLO Insider Tips

Our top 15 Insider Tips

INSIDER TIP **As romantic as it gets**
Take the boat from Dalyan after night has fallen and the silvery waves glitter in the moonlight; sail to İztuzu Beach where you can swim under the stars or just lie in the sand and watch the heavens → p. 36

INSIDER TIP **Giving 'Hell' as miss**
The two caves near Silifke are known as 'Heaven and Hell' (Cennet ve Cehennem) – but, you are only allowed to enter 'Heaven' → p. 91

INSIDER TIP **For the wild at heart**
Rafting is now popular at many places in Southern Turkey and the River Dalaman is especially suited for it. The instructor will tell you what to do and you can choose between various levels of difficulty. Life jackets must always be worn → p. 42

INSIDER TIP **The dream of flying**
You take off from Babadağ near Fethiye on your paraglider – alone or with your teacher in a new microlight – with the Mediterranean glittering below you. Thousands come here every year to float down from the almost 2000 m (6560 ft) high mountain (photo above) → p. 41

INSIDER TIP **Some like it hot**
And you will too when you bathe in the Sultaniye Kaplicalari, the sulphurous hot springs on the shore of Lake Köyceğiz (photo right) → p. 38

INSIDER TIP **Splash, splash!**
The Aquapark in Antalya is not only an exhilerating place for children to have fun → p. 104

INSIDER TIP **Up hill and down dale**
Through the mountains on your mountainbike: the proprietors of the Arykandos Mountain Lodge near Kaş provide training and guided tours → p. 63

INSIDER TIP **Dining with a view**
You will eat well and have a wonderful view of the sea in the first-class 7 Mehmet Restaurant in Antalya → p. 53

BEST OF ...

GREAT PLACES FOR FREE
Discover new places and save money

FOR FREE

● *Swimming with the turtles*
İztuzu Beach, where loggerhead sea turtles lay their eggs, is located between the freshwater delta of the River Dalyan and the Mediterranean. The canal is teeming with baby turtles, fish and crabs, and you can swim and snorkel with them to your heart's content → p. 35

● *Testimony to past life*
Greeks used to live in the small town of Kayaköy in Fethiye's hinterland. It was abandoned after a population exchange agreement was made after the Greco–Turkish War. The *Open Air Museum* boasts many fine examples of Greek architecture. Admission is free → p. 44

● *Sea, as far as the eye can see*
The *hill fortress in Alanya* is an ideal place to get an impression of the sea and countryside. Admission is free to visit the fortress almost 300 m above the Mediterranean and admire the view. Armed with a book and camera, you will never be bored up here → p. 72

● *Sunken palaces*
Admission to the *Underwater Museum* is free: Lycian graves and city remains lie near and under the water in Kekova close to Kaş. After the boat trip, you can take a swim and dive to explore the ruins → p. 65

● *At the waterfall*
It is always a delight to go for a walk and have a picnic near a peaceful river with or without a waterfall; if you are brave enough, you can even dive into the icy spring water. At *Düden Şelalesi* you can while away a wonderful day without spending any money (photo) → p. 57

● *The temple greets the sun*
The restored *remains of the Temple of Apollo* in Side rise up above the sea and are open to all No matter whether you come in the early morning to see the sunrise or watch the sun set in the evening – it is an unforgettable sight → p. 77

●●●● Dots in guidebook refer to 'Best of ...' tip

ONLY ON THE SOUTH COAST
Unique experiences

● *Hiking in the footsteps of ancient civilisations*

The chain of mountains running parallel to the Turkish Riviera offers many opportunities for short or long hikes. The *Lycian Way* is relatively new and well signposted. You can hike the entire trail or sections of it → p. 97

● *'Blue Voyage'*

You drop anchor from one of the old *wooden 'gulet' sailing boats* in Fethiye. The route takes you along the coast or to the Greek islands of Symi and Rhodes. You can decide whether you just want to swim or go on shore from one day to the next. The chefs are famous for their excellent cooking and the *raki* tastes good too (photo) → p. 42

● *Pretty as a picture*

The sea seems almost too beautiful to be true at many places on the south coast. Nothing can compare with the magnificent blueish-green water in front of the backdrop of pine forests in *Ölüdeniz Bay* near Fethiye → p. 45

● *Sunshine reggae*

At night, the old *yacht marina* in *Marmaris* and the streets behind it turn into an open-air discotheque. People go out well-dressed for their evening drink → p. 47

● *Oriental flair*

The *Kaleiçi* acts as a magnet for all holiday-makers on the south coast. The historical city centre of Antalya has many lovely boutique hotels, cafés and restaurants. It is a real delight just to sit at the marina and watch the hustle and bustle → p. 52

● *Deep blue*

Divers from all over the world flock to Kaş in summer. The charming small coastal town has developed into an *underwater sports Mecca* with excellent diving sites and schools → p. 63

● *A visit to the first Christians*

Paul the Apostle and his early Christian community have left traces along the south-east coast. Mass in the *Church of St Peter the Apostle* in Antakya is an unforgettable experience → p. 88

ONLY IN

BEST OF ...

● **Off to the museum!**
You should hope for a rainy day if you feel it's a shame going to a museum when the sun is shining. Anybody who does not visit the *Archaeological Museum in Antalya* has really missed out on something ... (photo) → p. 52

● **Shopping under cover**
If it rains, the *Migros Shopping Centre* in Antalya is a good place to spend some time. The Turks love this roofed bazaar. Apart from shops you can also find fast-food restaurants here as well as more fashionable cafés where you can sit and read the newspaper in peace → p. 54

● **Well and truly wet**
Go to a *hamam* – two or three hours will fly by if you take the full treatment. The old bath in the market in Fethiye is one with a very special atmosphere → p. 40

● **Dusty treasures**
The *Archaeological Museum in Adana* is the oldest museum in Turkey. The old-fashioned way in which the exhibits are displayed has great charm → p. 83

● **Under the earth**
If you don't like the way things look above, just go underground! The stalactite cave *Köşekbükü* offers something different and the weather there never changes → p. 86

● **Under the trees**
When the sand on the beach is as wet as the sea, life in a campsite can actually be more fun than being in the hotel. It's great to be outside on the shore and yet under cover: the campsite in Kaş makes a perfect choice → p. 64

RAIN

RELAX AND CHILL OUT
Take it easy and spoil yourself

● *Mud treatment and hot baths*

Tens of thousands of visitors visit the *hot springs at Horozlar* near Dalyan every year. The medicinal mud dries on your body in the open air; after that, a bath in the 39° C (102° F) water is an indescribable sensation for all the senses → p. 37

● *Simple, clean and hospitable*

It has now become difficult to find a peaceful spot to relax an the beach; your dreams will come true in the hospitable *Badem Motel* on Palamutbüku Bay near Datça → p. 49

● *Pure luxury*

The award-winning *Hillside Su* design hotel is the top address for weary city dwellers. The offer is topped off with underwater jazz music in the big swimming pool. Lie down on the adults-only beach and do absolutely nothing – heaven is not far away → p. 56

● *Sweat in the hamam*

Relaxation, peeling and a massage: these are the highlights of a Turkish bath. After the pores have widened in the steam, the skin is scrubbed; this is finished off with a massage. One address to note is *Sefa Hamamı* in Antalya → p. 55

● *Classical music in an ancient theatre*

The classical music concerts as well as opera and ballet in the ancient theatre in *Aspendos* between Antalya and Manvgat are absolute highlights in the summer. The acoustics are fabulous – just relax and enjoy the experience ... → p. 78

● *Yoga and meditation*

The *Yoga Ashram* meditation centre stands prominently above the green valley of the small River Dim in Alanya's hinterland. Mobile phones, iPods, computers and televisions are taboo. The organic food and walks along the river with yoga exercise in the water not only purify the body but also the soul (photo) → p. 75

INTRODUCTION

DISCOVER THE SOUTH COAST OF TURKEY

Beaches as far as the eye can see. No matter whether you look to the right or left, or back over your shoulder: there is no end in sight to the beach at Patara. The fine sand stretches for miles and the dunes carry on for hundreds of yards inland. And there are no busy roads behind them, only the last stone remains of ancient Patara, a once-important harbour town. If the weather is clear, the view from the old Lycian city reaches over the sea and as far as the Taurus Mountains that only seem to be a stone's throw away.

Even though Patara is a very special gem, this combination of wide beach, ancient sites and the peaks of the Taurus Mountains that are snow-covered until early summer is typical of the Turkish Mediterranean coast. The mountain range stretches for around 600 km (375 mi) from the western Aegean to the eastern rim of the Mediterranean: always within sight of the sea. The coastal strip in front it is sometimes so narrow that it almost seems that the mountains are about to slide into the sea; sometimes it is miles wide and covered with cotton fields – along with its secluded beaches, picturesque

Photo: Beydaglan Bay

villages, cultural highlights and lively tourist centres, it is one of the most varied holiday landscapes in the entire Mediterranean region. Antalya is the heart of Turkey's Mediterranean coast. In the past twenty years, it has developed at a dizzy speed from a sleepy little town on the coast into a tourist metropolis. Although there has been a great deal of construction, the old city centre has been carefully restored to preserve its original charm. Antalya is good starting point for a swim at one of the beaches to the east, as well as the romantic, steep and rocky coast with small coves to the west.

> ## There's something for everyone on the South Coast of Turkey

Leaving Antalya to the east, you reach a large sandy beach on the outskirts of the city; this is the beginning of the 'Turkish Riviera'. This stretch of the coast between Antalya and Alanya is one of the most popular holiday destinations for visitors from many other European countries. The tourism infrastructure in this region is absolutely state-of the-art and offers everything from all-inclusive complexes and small hotels in historical towns such as Side, to campsites and guesthouses in Manavgat. The Turkish Riviera would not be complete without its historical sites such as the amphitheatre in Aspendos and the ruins in Termessos.

Alanya is the second largest city on this stretch of the coast after Antalya and is home to some 10,000 West Europeans – about half from Germany and Denmark – who are attracted to this Eastern Mediterranean town with the highest average mean

3000 BC
Foundation of Troy and other settlements on the coast

From 1200 BC
Greek colonies on the west and south coasts

333 BC
Alexander the Great conquers the Persians and secures Greek dominance

2nd century–2nd century AD
Greek towns and settlements experience their heyday

330 AD
The Romans drive the Greeks away; Byzantium becomes the capital of the Roman Empire

Sunbathing on Cleopatra Beach – well guarded by Alanya's Seljuk fortress

temperature. If you travel to further eastwards, you will soon reach places that have hardly been affected by tourism. The coast becomes steeper, wide beaches rarer, and the closest airport ever further away. This is where the people living on the coast make their money more from agriculture than catering to tourists.

The coast reaches its southern-most point at Anamur and beyond it lies the Bay of Adana – the most easterly section of the

> **In the footsteps of the early Christians**

Mediterranean. The bay is not suitable for swimming due to the large industrial ports at Mersin and İskenderun, the oil loading port of Yumurtalık and the swampy plains

1307 Founding of the Ottoman Empire

1453 Ottomans take Constantinople and rename the city Istanbul

1914–18 The Ottoman Empire loses World War I as a German ally; the victors occupy Asia Minor

1920–22 War of liberation led by Mustafa Kemal, known as Atatürk

1923 Foundation of the Turkish Republic

1939–45 Turkey remains neutral in World War II

at the mouth of the River Ceyhan. Things start to get interesting again at the end of the bay just before the Syrian border. The Turkish city of Antakya is the biblical town of Antioch where Paul founded the first Christian community.

A few miles to the west of Antalya, you will be able to admire the most spectacular landscape of the eastern Mediterranean. This is where the Taurus Mountains plummet from a height of up to 3000 m (9850 ft) almost perpendicularly into the sea; the coastline is broken up into countless bays that offer everything from beaches of sand and pebbles to high cliffs. There are still many club complexes at the beginning

Lycia – a destination for individualists

of the stretch near Kemer but further on you will discover a paradise for individual travellers. Secluded bays in Olympos, charming little guesthouses in Kaş and wide sandy beaches at Patara: the Lycian coast is a dream for all those who want to go out and explore the area.

The best known tourist area in Turkey after Antalya are Fethiye, Marmaris and Bodrum. Ölüdeniz, one of the most magnificent Mediterranean bays near Fethiye, the rock tombs and reed forests at Dalyan, the sailors' paradise in Gökova Bay and the almond groves on the Datça Peninsula: the western tip of the coast has surprises in store going far beyond the spectacular paragliding leap from the Babadağ and the finest marina in the eastern Mediterranean in Marmaris. There are legendary places such as Knidos, unspoilt fishing villages such as Bozburun as well as luxurious holiday complexes and exclusive hotels near Marmaris. One of the loveliest ways to get to know the south coast of Turkey is on board a large wooden boat, a 'gulet'. Cruises along the coast are known as 'Blue Voyages' and offer the purest form of relaxation. And, as an extra, you will discover bays and other areas along the coast that are still difficult to reach from the land because there are no roads or tracks.

The high season on the south coast runs from April to November. The temperature rarely sinks below 10°C in the winter months but there can be heavy rainfalls between December and March. However, when it is sunny in February it becomes warm enough for the hotels to open their outdoor pools. The sun shines all the time from May to September and in July and August the temperature can reach more then 40° C (104° F)

1945–50 Introduction of a multiparty system; entry into NATO

1960–80 Three military coups (1960, 1971, 1980); Cyprus crisis (1974)

2002 The electoral victory of the moderate Islamists (AKP) leads to a government with a stable majority

2005 The EU starts accession negotiations with Turkey

2007 The conservative Islamic AKP party wins parliamentary elections; Abdullah Gül is named President

Witness to a splendid past: Roman aqueduct in Aspendos

However, there is usually a breeze to make things more pleasant. The Turkish tourism industry has done a lot in the past few years to make the south coast not only an attractive destination as a classical beach holiday but also for tourists interested in culture, as well as winter holiday-makers.

Many ancient sites are better cared for than only a few years ago and are now easier to reach. Golf courses and hiking trails attract those who want an active holiday and prefer to avoid the hot sum-

Appealing in the off season too

mer months. And not least of all, many hotels now have attractive offers for guests from northern Europe who want to spend the winter in Turkey.

Of course, Turkey's Mediterranean coast also has its negative aspects. In spite of the government's assurances not to make the same common mistakes as in other areas of mass tourism, there has been some unsightly development. And the crowds in Marmaris and Side mean that the often-sung oriental hospitality is no longer what it once was. The locals have developed a professional relationship to their visitors – this is not surprising considering the millions of holiday-makers who come every year. However, this changes as soon as you get a little bit off the beaten track. If you leave your holiday complex behind you and set out to explore the countryside, you will discover peaceful villages where time seems to have come to a standstill and where the people who live there always have a moment for a chat, even if there are some problems with the language. Here, visitors are still treated as guests. Leave your holiday rep at the hotel and set out alone; you will soon discover that everybody is interested in you and will do all they can to help.

WHAT'S HOT

1 Şalgam Suyu

Healthy 'in' drink Şalgam has become totally trendy. The tangy vegetable juice is now being served in an increasing number of cool bars and discos in Alanya's party district near the port – sometimes mixed with alcohol. The drink is a must to accompany the typical Adana kebab. *Güneyiller* restaurants in Antalya prepare fresh şalgam *(Turgut Reis Cad. and Atatürk Bulvarı 88)*. You can even take the drink home with you – sometimes spiced up with chilli *(www.hacininsalgami. com.tr)*.

Made in Turkey 2

Very fashionable Turkish brands are not only popular in the fashion capital of Istanbul but also in glamour centres worldwide. Those who want to be ahead of the rest shop at *Vakko (Mithatsaraçoğlu Cad., Lütfiye Hanım Ap. 7A, Adana, www. vakko.com.tr)* or *Herry (Atatürk Cad. 74A, Adana)*. *Mavi (www.mavi.com, photo)* has cool jeans, pretty blouses and scarves; *Ipeykol* sells fashion you can wear in the office but which will also turn heads at the after-work party *(Ziya Paşa Bulvarı, Adana, www. ipekyol.com)*.

3 Eat in the river

Fish on your plate There is no better way to eat. You dine on platforms floating on a lake at the *Botanik* restaurant. What do they serve? Fish, of course *(Ulupinar, www.ulupinarbotanikrestaurant. com)*. *Havuzbasi Selale* and *Havuzbasi Selale 2* are also close to the water and they serve trout straight out of the river – as fresh as it gets *(Ulupinar, www.selale restoran.com)*.

There are a lot of things to discover on the south coast of Turkey. Here is our hand-picked selection

Dancing on the waves

Wakeboarding Surfing is old hat. Trendy water sports enthusiasts have discovered the wakeboard. And, the best thing is that you don't have to wait for the waves if you want to train – just go to the *Hip Notics* Cable Park, that has also hosted the world championships, where you will be pulled by a cable and electric motor and not do any harm to the environment. This will also make it possible for you to try out your first daring tricks *(Antalya, www.hip-notics.com, photo)*. Mustafa, the wakeboard trainer at the *Seaqueen* water sports school, will show you how to get on and off the board with ease *(in Akka Antedon Hotel, Beldibi)*.

Two days of design

Check into a designer's paradise They fly in from Izmir and Istanbul, London and Hamburg. Antalya's designer hotels have become popular weekend destinations for Europe's luxury-seeking travellers. *Hillside Su* is a designer's dream come true. The hotel has so many fascinating details from white leather sofas and pink lights in the hamam, to the disco lights in the lobby *(Konyaaltı, Antalya, www.hillsidesu.com, photo)*. The *Adam & Eve Hotel* (Iskele Mevkii, Belek, www.adamevehotels.com) is another dream in white. There is more colour – and unusual details such as brushes on the walls as artworks – in *The Marmara* in the coastal town. But a weekend is really not long enough for a stay here *(Lara Cad., Antalya, www.themarmara hotels.com)*.

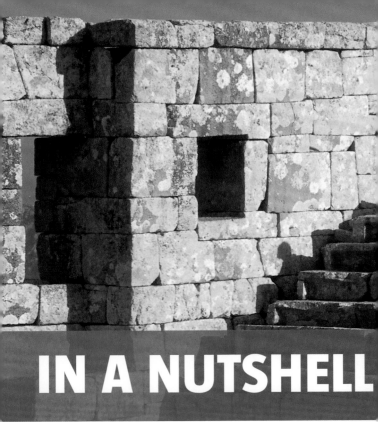

IN A NUTSHELL

ANTIQUITY

Anatolia's Mediterranean coast is one of the earliest known areas to have been settled. Excavations carried out near Çatal Hüyük between Antalya and Konya have unearthed Neolithic cultural objects including wall paintings and statues of bulls' heads from the seventh millennium BC. There is evidence that this region has been continuously inhabited during the thousands of years since then, as finds from the Bronze Age and Hittite period go to show. The ancient remains that can be visited today come from the time when the Greeks colonised the Anatolian coast and established settlements in 1200 BC.

Aspendos, Perge and Side are some of the most impressive testimonies to Greek culture that are still well preserved today.

ATATÜRK

Any visitor to Turkey who has a look around outside the hotel will notice the statues, busts and pictures of Mustafa Kemal Atatürk (1881–1938). Even the smallest towns have their Atatürk monument; there is no office and no bank hall that does not have at least one portrait hanging there. His honorary title 'Atatürk' ('Father of the Turks') is still justified today, as the modern republic founded in 1923 is largely his creation. He became famous

Photo: Termessos amphitheatre

A fact file on the Turkish south coast: society and history, culture and politics, religion and the economy

as a General in World War I and, following Turkey's defeat, organised the resistance against the occupation and partition of the Ottoman Empire among the victors. He became a national hero and leader of the War of Independence that the Turkish militia forces finally won. However, the most important phase of his activity began after the victory on the battlefield. Atatürk and his Republican People's Party (CHP)

decided to establish a laicist republic oriented on Europe. The last Ottoman sultan had to leave the country, Islam was abolished as the state religion, the Latin alphabet introduced and the language modernised. Atatürk introduced equal rights for women and forbade the wearing of typical Ottoman clothing such as the fez or a veil. Mustafa Kemal died in Istanbul at the age of 57. The problem with Atatürk's modernisation, so-called Kemalism, is that even today social change has been decreed from above and is not fully understood at some levels of society, especially in the countryside.

COTTON

You will sometimes find it hard to believe your eyes if you drive along the Mediterranean coast in autumn. The landscape is covered in a sea of white. But what looks like snow from a distance are actu-

While cotton is still picked by hand in many areas and there are masses of migrant workers on the roads in late summer, large field are now harvested by machine

CYPRUS

The largest island in the eastern Mediterranean is easy to reach from the Turkish coast. The rapid ferries only take about four hours for the crossing from Silifke to Girne, the most beautiful port town on the island. An international boy

A woman's work: harvesting the fields

ally cotton fields. The plant buds open up in autumn and release their small white balls of fibre. Cotton, 'white gold', is the most important source of income on the Mediterranean coast after tourism. It forms the basis of the Turkish textile industry and provides farmers with high profits. For this reason cotton almost developed into a monoculture in the area around Adana on the so-called Çukurova Plain.

cott has resulted in the Turkish-controlled northern section of Cyprus being relatively undeveloped for tourism although the landscape is among the most beautiful the Island of Aphrodite has to offer. A trip to Cyprus is well worthwhile and most tourists from western countries do not need a visa. Politically, Cyprus is a sad case. When the Greek Cypriots rejected a UN plan for the reunification of the island in 2004 only the Greek section was able to accede to the EU while the Turkish part remained isolated internationally. The border between the two sections has been opened for Cypriots at some places but tourists who travel to North Cyprus from Turkey are still not allowed to also visit the south.

EUROPEAN UNION

Will Turkey become a member – yes or no? This question has become increasingly pressing since accession negotiations began in 2005 because France and Germany have shown a more negative attitude towards Turkey's membership. This is further complicated by the dissent between the new EU member-state Cyprus and Turkey over the Turkish-settled north of the island that has still not been solved and has led to the Greek-Cypriot government repeatedly blocking negotiations. The fact that some EU countries reject Turkey's accession has led to the country's enthusiasm cooling off and to necessary reforms slowing down. The question of EU membership remains unanswered but those in favour on both sides are doing all they can to keep discussions moving.

FOOTBALL

Hardly anyone connects the Turkish Mediterranean coast with serious football but the beaches are an El Dorado for players. Professional teams from Northern Europe discovered Antalya and its surroundings a few years ago as an ideal training location during the winter. The climate is mild and just right for regaining stamina, the hotels often have first-class football grounds, and fitness training is much more fun on the beach than at home in the cold. The teams have become a steady source of income for hoteliers; they not only come with their trainers and other sidekicks, many of their fans also book a holiday in the same hotel.

ISLAM

Officially, Turkey is a secular republic. There is no state religion and religion should not play a role in government institutions. Islam was even strongly combated in the period of one-party government (see: Atatürk) until the end of World War II and partly forced underground. All this has changed greatly since then. Islam could already be noticed more strongly in public life in the 1980s and '90s, the restrictions against Islamic orders were lifted and religious instruction was reintroduced into state schools. Turkey has been ruled by a party that has its roots in political Islam since 2002. Since then, there has been a real clash of cultures between the AK Party and its supporters on the one hand and the secular population, mostly in the large cities, on the other. The covering of women's heads and bodies and a ban on alcohol are two of the prime concerns. There are plenty of heated discussions about both, and the conservatives seem to be gaining ground. But Turkey is nowhere near introducing Islamic law, the Sharia, or making Friday a holiday – as in other Islamic countries – instead of Sunday.

Visitors who spend most of their time on the coast or the other tourist centres in the country will hardly notice anything of this trend towards Islam. But, if you branch out and make an excursion to Anatolian cities in the interior, you will probably hardly find a restaurant that serves alcohol.

KURDS

The Kurds did not originally live on the Mediterranean. They come from further to the east, the mountainous region in the south-east of Turkey along the borders to Iran and Iraq. However, millions of Kurds moved to other areas after the foundation of the Republic and many of them settled in the area around Adana and Mersin. The illegal Kurdish Workers' Party (PKK) has been fighting and armed fued for an independent state for 20 years. More than 30,000 people have been killed and many farmers driven out of their villages. A shaky kind of peace has been in force in the Kurdish regions since the PKK boss Abdullah Öcalan was captured in 1999.

Mountains from Dalyan to Fethiye and Antalya. There are also several different types of isolated rock tombs. Although a relatively small nation, the Lycians must have been able to protect themselves successfully for many centuries against the major Anatolian power, the Hittites, as well as Greek colonists and Persian rulers from around the 15th to 3rd century BC. They were obviously so successful in de

Daring construction: Lycian rock tombs near Kale

LYCIANS
The Lycians were first mentioned in Homer's *Iliad* as the people who supported the Trojans. Archaeologists still know very little about their origins – in spite of the tombs they left as witnesses of their culture. The famous tombs of the Lycians can be found in the rock walls of the Taurus

fending their fortresses high up in the Taurus Mountains that no major ancient power was able to subjugate them.

PIRATES
Today, if you see a dazzling white sail shining in the sun out to sea, you know that a yacht is peacefully sailing through

the water. Things were different 2000 years ago. The Mediterranean was a pirate's paradise and the first thing people did then when they saw a sail on the horizon was to look for a safe haven. The Cilician coast, near to where Antalya stands today, was a stronghold of piracy. The most important port of the brotherhood of pirates – which formed large crews to capture ships and made sailing in the entire Mediterranean a dangerous affair in the 1st and 2nd centuries BC – was located there. The pirates sailed as far as the Adriatic and even went to mainland Italy and almost paralysed Roman maritime trade.

In 75 BC, Cilician pirates managed to take Julius Caesar himself prisoner. His ransom amounted to 50 talents – an enormous sum – but after his release, Caesar set out to pursue his abductors. General Pompey was given 20 legions, 500 ships and command over the entire Mediterranean. The pirates had no chance against such an armada. After a few months, Pompey had sunk the pirates' fleet and destroyed their strongholds on the Cilician coast.

TOURISM

For a decade, Turkey has belonged to the group of rapidly growing newly industrialised countries (NICs) on the threshold of becoming a fully-developed economic player. Turkey has an average growth rate of 7% and the Istanbul Stock Exchange is one of the most profitable worldwide. Although there is still quite a lot of poverty, consumption is continuously increasing and more and more Turks can afford a car and to take a summer holiday.

The tourism industry is one of the most important growth sectors in the country and regularly reports new successes. Antalya, the metropolis on the south coast, was one of the most-visited cities in the world in 2010: it ranked in fourth place behind Paris, London and Singapore. Of course, this includes the entire Antalya region that has become an increasingly popular tourist destination. Only a few years ago, visitors from European countries had Antalya almost to themselves but today Russians are challenging the German's number one position. Many tourist from Iran and the Gulf States have started visiting now that Turkey has done away with visa requirements for travellers from most Arab countries. However, Arabs from the wealthy Gulf States are more interested in Istanbul than sandy beaches. They can combine the pleasures available in a western city with the customs of an Islamic land in the metropolis on the Bosporus, and this has now become a great attraction for visitors from the Middle East.

WOMEN

Turkish women enjoy legal equality and have been eligible to vote since 1930. Although there are few legal restrictions on women participating in public life, they are frequently confronted with a traditional, patriarchal mindset in their everyday activities. This is particularly true in rural areas, in the poor immigrant districts on the outskirts of the large cities, and in the east of Turkey. In recent years family law has been adapted to meet western European standards and women now also have full equality in marriage. The fact that there are still cases of child marriages and illegal polygamy in conservative religious circles is a sign of the great differences in the development of a country that has been subject to rapid changes over the past few decades. However, unlike other Islamic countries, female tourists will not find themselves subjected to any kind of restrictions at all.

FOOD & DRINK

As is the case with so many other things in Turkey, the cuisine is actually a synthesis. **Turkish herdsmen brought milk products such as yoghurt with them from Central Asia. Byzantine fish and poultry dishes were taken over and sophisticated starters with walnuts and chickpeas introduced from Arab countries.**

Wheat came from Mesopotamia and was baked into the white bread that is popular throughout Turkey. Immigrants from Russia and the Balkans brought pastries *(börek)* with them and, last but not least, the Mediterranean provided fresh fruit and vegetables, herbs and olives. You will still find all of these on the menus of good restaurants. And it is well known that the so-called 'Mediterranean diet' with vegetable oil and more white than red meat can actually lengthen one's lifespan! It is a fact that heart and vascular illnesses, cancer and diabetes, are less common around the Mediterranean than in Northern European countries. The cuisine you find on the south cast of Turkey ranges from Aegean cooking similar to that in Greece in the west to the very oriental, Arab style of food in the east in the area around Adana and Antakya. The further east you travel the spicier and fattier the food becomes. But, wherever you are, you will always find light salads, fresh yoghurt and fruit.

Photo: Restaurant near the port in Antalya

Choose between fresh vegetables and fish, a great variety of fruit and pure vegetable oils – the food you eat here is really healthy

The Turkish breakfast offers more then the continental but less than the British variety. The holiday villages and large hotels usually serve lavish breakfast buffets, but elsewhere you will always find butter, sheep's cheese, jam, honey, olives, tomatoes and cucumbers. In the countryside, farmers will offer you olive oil with thyme *(kekik)* for you to dip your bread into. Turks drink tea *(çay)* in the morning. You will be served instant coffee with milk *(sütlü)* or without *(sade)*. Seeing that the main meal is served in the evening and most hotels offer half-board, you will have to still your hunger somewhere else at lunchtime. There are many cafés in all holiday resorts where you can buy snacks such as pizzas, omelettes, crêpes and sandwiches. The stone ovens in the kebab houses are already hot so that you won't have to wait very long for

LOCAL SPECIALITIES

▶ **arnavut ciğeri** – fresh, finely sliced lamb's liver ('Albanian style'), dipped in flour and fried

▶ **Çercez tavuğu** – 'Circassian chicken' is a sophisticated appetiser prepared with walnuts

▶ **çoban salata** – tomatoes, chillies, cucumber, onions and black olives, at least, have to be included in any decent shepherd's salad

▶ **çupra ızgara** – grilled sea perch is only found on the Mediterranean

▶ **deniz börülcesi** – 'sea beans' only grow in untouched bays and are eaten raw with olive oil

▶ **gözleme** – crêpes filled with cheese or minced meat

▶ **haydari** – a thick spread made of sheep's cheese, yoghurt, parsley, chillies, mint and garlic

▶ **iç pilav** – this royal Ottoman dish comprises rice with currants, tomatoes, chicken liver and pine nuts spiced with cinnamon

▶ **kazandibi** – made of milk, rice flour and vanilla sugar, should scorch a little first to taste really good

▶ **kılıçbaliği şişte** – spicy, marinated swordfish, grilled on a skewer, with peppers and onions

▶ **künefe** – an Arabian dessert: cheese baked in the oven with sugar

▶ **mantı** – Turkish tortellini filled with minced meat and served covered with garlic yoghurt (photo right)

▶ **midye dolması** – mussels filled with *iç pilav* and served cold

▶ **oruk** – this famous dish from Antakya looks like a big, golden-brown roasted Easter egg and is made of minced meat, bulgur, flour, hot spices and oil. The ingredients are kneaded and grilled in the oven

▶ **pacinga böreği** – vol-au-vents filled with air-dried cured beef *(pastırma)*

▶ **sebze borani** – *borani* are specialities of Antakya. The vegetables (such as spinach or chickpeas) are usually prepared with minced meat, yoghurt and garlic

▶ **sıcak helva** – sesame nougat fried in a pan: a delicious dessert! (photo left)

▶ **tarator** – creamy, pink spread of fish eggs, very filling

▶ **zeytinyağli enginar** – artichoke hearts with oil, served with carrots and potatoes

your Turkish 'pizza' with minced meat *(lahmacun)* or flatbread *(pide)* with cheese *(peynirli),* mince *(kıymalı),* thin slices of meat *(kuşbaşi etli),* turkish ham *(pastırmalı)*

FOOD & DRINK

with beaten egg (*yumurtalı*) or without (*yumurtasız*). *Ayran*, a yoghurt drink, is the right accompaniment but, be careful, it can make you tired! Wherever you see the famous revolving spit – the doner kebab – you will also be able to get *ıskender* (with tomato sauce and butter) or simply ask for a sandwich to eat with your hands. There are also skewers with Turkish ham (*sucuk*) or chicken (*tavuk*) – the former is spicy, the latter a bit dry without tomato sauce (*domates sosu*).

In the evening, people usually take their place at the table shortly before sunset. Aperitifs are only customary in the large hotels and holiday villages. Imported beverages are more expensive than local drinks. It is a better idea to drink *Efes Pilsen* beer than foreign ales, and Aegean wines rather than those from overseas. Considerable advances have been made in wine production in recent years: *Antik*, *Angora* and *Sarafin* can all be recommended. Water is always non-carbonated; with bubbles, it is known as *soda*. It is a good idea to drink the potent aniseed liquor *rakı* only in small doses!

There are five courses to the classical Turkish dinner. It begins with cold starters (*meze*) such as aubergine purée (*patlıcan salata*), *humus* (a mixture of chickpeas, oil and garlic), octopus salad (*ahtapot salatası*), pickled fish (*lakerda, çiroz*), spicy tomato purée with peppers (*ezme*) or stuffed vine leaves (*sarma*), sheep's cheese (*beyaz peynir*), melon (*kavun*), green salad (*göbek salata*) and shepherd's salad (*çoban salata*). This is followed by a selection of warm appetisers that can include rolls of pastry with sheep's cheese (*sigara böreği*), lamb's liver and onions (*arnavut ciğeri*), fried mussels (*midye tava*) and calamari (*kalamar*). Shrimp served in a clay pot (*karides güveç*) is especially tasty. The main course is usually a choice between meat and fish; vegetarians should

Ottoman culinary culture: a corner in a traditional restaurant

simply continue with the starters. Meat is most often served grilled: lamb chops (*pirzola*), skewered lamb (*şiş kebab*) or steaks (*bonfile, külbastı*) are sprinkled with thyme; rice (*pilav*) is a common side dish. Freshly-caught fish is usually displayed in a refrigerated showcase at the entrance; always ask about the price before you order. You will hardly find fish in the south east and will have to be satisfied with meat.

Desserts are usually the national sweet dishes such as *baklava* (pastry with nuts) and *helva* (nougat) – both are extremely sugary. After this, fresh fruit is often served and the meal comes to an end with a small cup of strong Turkish coffee.

Restaurants are open every day during the high season (June–Sept) but quite a few in the tourist hotspots close from October to May. In the interior of the country, many restaurants are closed during the day in the fasting month of Ramadan (at a different time every year) and only open shortly before sunset.

SHOPPING

The more a bazaar caters to tourists, the shoddier the goods. This rule applies to the main holiday centres such as Side and Kemer. Another rule to consider: prices rise in the high season. This applies to leather jackets just as it does to apples and pears. And, another tip: groceries are cheaper in the evening; valuable goods such as carpets leather clothing and jewellery, on the other hand, are less expensive in the morning. The merchants are pleased to have their first customer and believe that they will have luck throughout the day if he doesn't leave the shop empty handed. Carpets, kilims, leatherwear and gold and silver jewellery are the most popular articles.

CARPETS

Extremely valuable carpets are woven in the mountains of the inland district away from the coast. Your hotel in Antalya or Adana will be able to give you information. If you decide to buy a carpet, you can settle on the price by talking with your hands. Most tourists will choose to shop in towns. You should pay attention to the number of knots per square centimetre –

the more knots, the more valuable the carpet. Ask for carpets and kilims made with naturally-dyed wool; aniline dyes often run when they get wet. If you don't trust the salesperson's information, you can usually take a carpet with you and get a second opinion – but only do that if you really intend to buy it later! The same applies to bargaining: you can frequently beat the price down to around 75 percent of what was originally asked. But, if you don't want to buy, you should not even start haggling The dealers will send the carpets to your home free of charge. If you take the carpet with you, keep the bill to show at customs

GOLD & SILVER

Gold is less expensive in Turkey than in EU countries. The 22-carat, richly gleaming precious metal is the highest-quality but of course, also the most expensive. Jewellers display the current gold price in their windows. There is a wider selection of 18-carat gold jewellery that you are accustomed to from home, and it is cheaper. It is also possible to barter here. But, be careful: many minerals and stones are manipulated in

In Turkey, shopping is something of a ritual: first you look, then bargain, drink a cup of tea, chat and then continue bargaining

various ways to improve their qualities (colour, brilliance, durability) and make them look like other, rare, more precious gems (such as turquoise).

HERBS

Wonderfully aromatic medicinal and kitchen herbs – thyme, basil, mint and many others – grow on the slopes of the Taurus Mountains further inland from the Mediterranean coast. The leaves are picked every day and taken to the herb shop owner, the *aktar*, in the market districts. They sell special mixtures for bronchitis, rheumatism, sleeplessness and even to ease depression. The *aktar's* knowledge has been handed down from grandfather to father to son for generations and it is well worth visiting such a shop – if only to buy delicious sun-dried tomatoes for your spaghetti sauce when you get back home.

In the meantime, there is even a range of natural Turkish make-up. The creams made by the *Bosphorus* and *Cemre* companies are especially recommendable.

TEXTILES

If you are on the lookout for authentic, hand-woven material coloured with vegetable dyes, you are bound to find what you want on the south coast of Turkey. Magnificent pure cotton material – sold by the metre or in the form of tablecloths and napkins – is especially cheap at the weekly markets. There are shops in the market districts of small towns such as Fethiye and Alanya that specialise in these goods. You will be able to find good, inexpensive bath and beach towels in shops that sell typical household goods for the bottom drawer – they can be recognised by the lingerie and linens in their windows.

THE PERFECT ROUTE

FROM DATÇA TO ÖLÜDENIZ

The ① *Reşadiye Peninsula* → p. 48 juts out to the west into the Aegean Sea like a long finger. You can take a boat from *Datça*, the largest town on the peninsula, to the ancient ruins of *Knidos* at the western tip. The entire peninsula still offers a great deal of pristine countryside. Especially towards the north at Gökova Bay, a fjord that reaches almost 100 km (62 mi) inland, there are many hiking trails through the pine forests down to the sea. On the way to the west, you reach the next tourist hotspot ② *Marmaris* → p. 46. Although it has now developed into a sprawling town, Marmaris is still surrounded by forests and skirts one of the most sheltered large bays on the Turkish coast. It is possible to swim in the turquoise-coloured water in the nearby small coves until winter. Its splendid location has made Marmaris the largest sailing marina in Turkey. This is the right place for holiday-makers who want to charter a boat to explore the coast. There are several buses to ③ *Fethiye* → p. 39 every day. According to Turkish tourist brochures the most beautiful beach in the country is to be found at *Ölüdeniz Bay* → p. 45. You can also make a spectacular descent on a paraglider from the almost 2000 m (6500 ft) high Mount *Babadağ* down into the bay. Along with Marmaris, Fethiye is *the* port for 'Blue Voyages' on a wooden sailing boat.

THROUGH LYCIA TO ANTALYA

The divers' paradise ④ *Kaş* → p. 62 is located to the south-east of Fethiye in an area that is still hardly touched by tourism. Every day boats set out to sea from this idyllic little town to take diving enthusiasts to the bays of Kekova. Kaş lies in the centre of the ancient area of Lycia and ⑤ *Kekova* → p. 65 is a sunken Lycian city that can be explored underwater. The road from Kaş passes ⑥ *Olympos* → p. 68 (photo above) on its way to the main city on the Mediterranean coast, ⑦ *Antalya* → p. 51. The city has grown rapidly in recent years and its airport boasts the highest number of passengers. *Kaleiçi*, the old city of Antalya from Seljuk times, lies behind the ancient city walls and seems far removed from the hectic activity of the tourist metropolis. The wooden houses around the historical port are gems of old Turkish architecture.

Experience all of the facets of the south coast of Turkey from the Reşadiye Peninsula in the west to Antakya in the east

ON THE TURKISH RIVIERA

The stretch of coast from Antalya to Alanya is known as the Turkish Riviera. The Temple of Apollo in ⑧ *Side* → p. 76 – a seaside resort that was very popular even in ancient times – lies in its centre. There are endless beaches near Side. The River Köprü has cut ravines, some of them as more than 300ft high, through *Köprülü Canyon* (photo left). The former Seljuk fortress dominates the landscape high above ⑨ *Alanya* → p. 70. If you have had enough of the hustle and bustle of the Riviera, you will find something quite different further east. Turkish holiday-makers still have ⑩ *Anamur* → p. 84, the southernmost point on the coast, almost entirely to themselves. There you will come across peaceful holiday settlements and small towns in banana plantations; old fortresses and the green hinterland provide a tranquil setting for relaxation.

BARBAROSSA AND ST PETER

The Holy Roman Emperor Frederick I Barbarossa drowned in the River Göksu, not far from today's ⑪ *Silifke* → p. 89, in 1190. Today, the path along the river from Silifke is a pleasant hike. A monument in his honor may be found on the Silifke–Mut road. ⑫ *Antakya* → p. 86, the biblical town of Antioch, is located at the eastern end of the Turkish Mediterranean coastline. It is now a pleasant provincial city with a mosaic museum which provides a good impression of its former Roman splendour, and one of the earliest Christian churches anywhere, the Church of St Peter the Apostle. This is a spot where traces of the oldest civilisations of the orient converge.

Approx. 1300 km (810 mi), travel time: around 24 hours. A detailed map of the route can be found on the back cover, in the road atlas and on the pull-out map

THE SOUTHWEST COAST

The southwest coast of Turkey, which includes the 100 km (62 mi) long Datça Peninsula at the tip of which the Aegean meets the Mediterranean, is a paradise for those who love sailing, swimming and snorkeling. This is where the 'Blue Voyage', a peaceful sailing trip on traditional wooden boats from bay to bay, was invented.

The coast is extremely rugged and provides many wonderful bays – which can only be reached by land with great difficulty – to drop anchor in. In addition to the large Gökova Gulf that reaches more than 100 km (62 mi) inland, the fjord-like bays in Marmaris, Ekincik and Fethiye make this section of the coast particularly attractive.

Although three of the main tourist destinations in Turkey, Marmaris, Fethiye and Bodrum (at the western tip of the Gulf of Gökova), are located in this region, there are still countless delightful places and sights that mass tourism has not yet discovered. Visitors who prefer to explore this coastal area by car or bus instead of from the water will also have plenty of opportunities to discover impressive natural and cultural monuments. A trip along Lake Köyceğiz, one of the most beautiful nature reserves in Turkey, is an unforgettable experience.

Photo: Ölüdeniz Bay near Fethiye

In the 'Blue Voyage' region: the southwestern section of the Turkish Mediterranean coast offers beaches, sports and a lot of fun

Holiday-makers wanting a change from the solitude of isolated bays will find plenty of ways to amuse themselves in Marmaris, Fethiye and Dalyan. From shopping to an evening at the disco, everything can be found in these large centres, as well as first-rate hotels and good restaurants catering for every taste. Many airlines have direct flights to the region's international airport in Dalaman.

DALYAN

(125 E5) *(ɲ E6)* **The former fishing village of Dalyan (pop. 5000; 35,000 in summer) only developed into a small, high-class, tourist resort in recent decades.**

In contrast to most other holiday resorts, Dalyan is not on the sea but on a canal that links Lake Köyceğiz with the

A must for holidaymakers in Fethiye: a boat trip through the reed delta

Mediterranean. A little behind Dalyan, the canal widens to a form a large delta covered with floating islands of reeds that can reach a height of 3 metres and you feel like you are in a labyrinth on the boat trip to the beach through the ★ *reed delta*. Dalyan became famous as the centre of an endeavour to protect the threatened loggerhead sea turtle *Caretta caretta*. The turtles that swim in the canal (so-called Nile turtles) do not belong to the caretta species and feed on fish.

The area around Dalyan as far as Köyceğiz was declared a nature reserve with strict building regulations in 1998. This has protected Dalyan from ugly hotel blocks and has made it possible to preserve the characteristic charm of the town in spite of an increasing number of visitors. The locals live mainly from fishing and cotton. Hotels, holiday flats and restaurants line the left bank of the river. From some places, tourists can see the Lycian rock tombs that were carved into the steep slope of the mountain on the other side of the river.

SIGHTSEEING

KAUNOS ★
The ruins of the ancient city of Kaunos, a settlement whose heyday was in the 4th century BC, are located opposite Dalyan. At the time, Kaunos was a harbour city on the border between Caria and Lycia – famous for salted fish and slave trading. Homer mentions the town but also notes that it had an unhealthy climate due to the many swamps in the area; this probably means that malaria was widespread. Those who feel up to it, should climb up to the Kaunos ⚡ *acropolis* at a height of 152 m (499 ft) and admire the fantastic panoramic view over the estuary delta to the beach and the cast expanse of Lake Köyceğiz. The well-preserved *theatre* with 33 rows of seats is located below the acropolis and a path leads from it down to the *harbour* that became silted up almost 2000 years ago. You can either take a boat from Dalyan to the other side and walk past the Lycian tombs over the hill

to Kaunos or sail directly to the new port of Kaunos. *Daily 8.30am–5.30pm | entrance fee 6.25 lira*

RADAR TOWER ☆

Magnificent observation spot: leaving Dalyan in the direction of İztuzu Beach, turn off the road around 1 km before the junction and head up to the radar tower from where you have an unbelievable view over the entire delta. You can even see as far as the Sandras Mountains beyond Lake Köyceğiz. The road continues to Asi Bay, a popular stopover on the 'blue voyage'. This is the place to take a swim far away from the crowds – sometimes, you will even be completely alone.

FOOD & DRINK

CEYHAN ☆

This restaurant on a meadow directly on the water is made even more attractive by its view across the canal towards the rock tombs that are floodlit at night. The menu lists fish and meat dishes as well as vegetable starters. Quiet. *Daily | Gülpinar Mah. Sahil Kenan | tel. 0252 2 84 21 29 | Moderate*

DENIZATI

The 'Seahorse', where fish from the local cooperative is served, is the best restaurant in Dalyan. There is also grilled meat and an excellent selection of appetisers. *Kordon Kenarı | tel. 0252 2 84 20 57 | Moderate*

KÖŞEM

Köşem Restaurant with its lovely garden is very popular in summer and serves local specialities such as blue crabs. This crustaceans have more meat than normal freshwater crayfish and turns red when grilled. *Daily | Liman Cad. 149 (in the market area) | tel. 0252 2 84 22 22 | Moderate*

INSIDER TIP ▶ SAKI

Family-run restaurant at a peaceful spot on the river. Excellent Turkish cuisine. *Maraş Mah. Sağlik Ocaği Yanı | tel. 0252 2 84 52 12 | Budget*

BEACHES

Dalyan's ● *İztuzu Beach* is one of the most beautiful in all of Turkey. However, the beach is closed to visitors after 8pm to protect the endangered loggerhead sea turtles that lay their eggs here. The best way to reach İztuzu is by boat from Dalyan. Almost all the hotels offer a boat service to the beach or you can take a *dolmuş* boat – a kind of maritime shared taxi – from the port *(fare around 3.75 lira)*. The

MARCO POLO HIGHLIGHTS

DALYAN

INSIDER TIP moonlight tours to İztuzu Beach, where you can swim at night, depart from the quay.

LEISURE & SPORTS

You can visit Kaunos on your own initiative to watch the 150 various species of birds living in the nature reserve. Start out early in the morning. The boats dock at the quay. It is a good idea to agree on the price with the fishermen on the previous day and make a deposit to reserve the boat.

ENTERTAINMENT

JAZZ BAR
The bar at the end of the marina has been there for almost two decades. There is live music on Mondays, Wednesdays and at the weekend; jazz, blues and rock. The prices are moderate. *Daily from 9pm | Gülpinar Mah. 30 | tel. 0542 3 71 65 85*

ROCK BAR
This is where lovers of good rock music meet. Dim lighting and always a great atmosphere. Needless to say it can get rather loud here! *Daily 8am–3am | Maraş Mahallesi Barlar Meydanı*

WHERE TO STAY

DALYAN HOTEL
The oldest hotel in Dalyan has 20 simple, spotless rooms and lies on a promontory opposite the tombs. Pool, restaurant, hotel boat to the beach. *20 rooms | Maraş Mah. Yalı Sokak | tel. 0252 2 84 22 39 | www.hoteldalyan.com | Moderate*

HAPPY CARETTA HOTEL
Wonderfully located, friendly hotel on the river with a view towards the rock tombs. Families welcome. Lovely garden, boat to the beach. *18 rooms | Maraş Cad. Kaunos Sok. 26 | tel. 0252 2 84 21 09 | www.happycaretta.com | Moderate–Expensive*

KILIM HOTEL
Comfortable, with a large garden and pool; peaceful, pleasant atmosphere; multilingual proprietors. *16 rooms | Kaunos Sokak 7 | tel. 0252 2 84 22 53 | www.kilimhotel.com | Budget–Moderate*

NATURAL VILLA APARTMENTS
The apartments are in a pretty new building with a swimming pool only 50 m from the canal. Air-conditioned holiday flats with kitchen, bathroom and balcony. *Gülpinar*

THE TURTLES' GODMOTHER

June Haimoff came to Dalyan in 1975 at the age of 53 on her small sailing boat 'Bouboulina'. She discovered İztuzu Beach at the time, left it, only to return eight years later and build a wooden hut there. One night, she discovered the caretta turtles laying their eggs. When plans were made to build a large hotel here at the end of the 1980s, she started her battle to protect the breeding place of the rare turtles. The German newspaper 'Tageszeitung' publicised her struggle and this contributed to her ultimate success – construction of the hotel was prevented. The Turks now lovingly call her 'Captain June'; she has stayed in Dalyan and became a Turkish citizen in 2009.

Mahallesi | tel. 0252 2 84 28 26 | www. natural-villa.com | Moderate

PORTAKAL

Charming hotel on the river. Shady bar in the garden, large pool. A shuttle boat takes guests to the beach. *45 rooms | Maraş Mah. Dalko Karşısı | tel. 0252 2 84 44 41 | www.hotelportakal.com | Budget*

WHERE TO GO

ÇAMUR BANYOLARI (MUD BATHS) ●
(125 E5) (*ω E6*)
If you go a little more than half a mile upstream from Dalyan instead of downstream to the beach, you will reach the *Horozlar* mud baths *(Çamur Banyoları)*. These are hot, sulphurous springs that bubble out of the earth at the foot of the mountain. You can give yourself a mudpack or just have a good time splashing around in the warm water. There is a regular boat service from Dalyan to the hot springs. *Entrance fee approx. 12 lira.*

EKINCIK (125 E5) (*ω D6*)
The little village of Ekincik, and especially the bay of the same name, are absolute gems that are very popular with yachting enthusiasts. The easiest way to reach Ekincik from Dalyan is by boat along the coast to the west passing İztuzu Beach (about 1 hour). Ekincik lies at the end of the fjord-like bay. If you moor half way into the bay on the right, you can climb up steep flight of steps to one of the most beautiful restaurants on the entire coast:
★ *My Marina (tel. 0252 2 66 02 76 |*

Expensive). The lovely *Ekincik Butik Hotel (27 rooms | tel. 0252 2 66 02 03 | www. hotelekincik.com | Moderate)* is located at the end of the bay.

It is also possible to hike from Dalyan to Ekincik Bay. First of all, you have to cross from the quay where the boats leave for the rock tombs. That is where the road begins that takes you past ancient Kaunos

Mudpack in the Çamur Banyoları

to the village of Çandır. The signposted path offers magnificent views and ends in Ekincik Bay. The hike will take around three hours and you can travel back by boat. The pine trees that seem to have white manes that you will see along the way are actually covered with bird droppings. This is where eagles threatened with extinction still nest in mountain crevices.

KÖYCEĞIZ (125 E5) (*ω E5*)
The almost 19⅓ mi² Lake Köyceğiz inland from Dalyan was once a sea bay that silted up in ancient times. Its water is fed through the canal and is slightly salty making it possible for sea fish to live here.

DALYAN

The first settlements were established in 3400 BC; Scythians, Assyrians, Ionians, Dorians, Persians, Hellenes, Romans and finally the Ottomans have all left their traces in the mountains around the lake. The small town has a provincial, very Turkish and extremely peaceful air. There are small hotels and guesthouses includ-

LOW BUDGET

▶ You can start your day with stretching and pilates at the pool of the *Kilim Hotel* in Fethiye for 5 lira a day. The after-sport coffee is free. *Babatasi Mah., Mustafa Kemal Bulvari, Karayollari Karsisi | tel. 0252 12 45 54 | www.hotelkilim.be*

▶ Luxury hotel complexes may be prohibitively expensive most of the time but there are many last-minute offers – often at half-price. For example, families with young children will be especially happy in *Club Lykia World* in the off-season (April/May, Oct). *269 rooms | Kidrak Mevkii | Ölüdeniz-Fethiye | tel. 0252 6 17 02 00 | www.lykiaworld.com*

▶ If you stay in *Midas Pension* in Dalyan, you will be able to sit on a 5 wooden terrace above the river and look at the Lycian rock tombs – and that, for around 62 lira a day. *10 rooms | Selçuk Nur, prop. | tel. 0252 2 84 | www.dalyanturkey.com*

▶ Not only the pub district in Marmaris celebrates happy hour between 5pm or 6pm and 7pm or 8pm – then, a large beer only costs around 5 lira.

ing the *Panorama Plaza* with a lovely garden and outdoor pool *(28 rooms, 4 suites |Ulucamii Mah. | Cengiz Topel Cad. 69 | tel. 0252 2 62 37 73 | www.panorama-plaza.de/de/englisch/frame_eng.html | Moderate)* on the outskirts. There is a fascinating village market in Közceğiz on Mondays. Anglers do not need a license to try their luck – bait and hooks for the local mullet *(kefal)* are available on the quay. The water is not very clear but is suitable for swimming. There is a small beach at the east of the strip of coast with liquidambar trees behind it, shower cabins and a kiosk.

Köyceğiz is also well known for its hot springs, the **INSIDER TIP** *Sultaniye Kaplicalari*. The radioactive medicinal springs that were already used in the Byzantine period bubble out of the earth at the foot of the Ölemez Hill on the south-west side of the lake. There is a domed roof over the springs and there is also an outdoor pool for mud treatment, changing rooms, showers, a restaurant and relaxation rooms. The baths in the 39–42° C (102–108° F) warm water are said to help against rheumatism, lumbago, skin diseases and nervous disorders. Boats leave from the quay for the springs in the morning and return in the early afternoon.

SARIGERME (125 E6) *(ᗰ E6)*

Its proximity to Dalaman Airport has led to Sarigerme developing into a top tourist destination in recent years. There is now a beach of fine sand underneath a blue sky that is cloudless for nine months of the year where the ancient city of Physilis once stood. The village of *Osmaniye*, around ½ mi inland, was where timber used for centuries for ship building, was brought to. *Baba Island*, opposite the gently sloping, shallow-water beach which is 7 km (4½mi) long can easily be reached by good swimmers. Boats anchor on the beach side of the island whereas the rocky side is a paradise for divers. There are bed & breakfasts and guesthouses in the village as well as 5-star complexes such as the *Hilton* or *Robinson Club*. It is easy to hike to the *Kapıdağ Peninsula* from here where you can visit the ruins of the Lycian cities of *Kyra*, *Lissai* and *Lydai*.

excavated behind the port. It is an early-Roman construction and was renovated in the 2nd century BC. With seating for 5000 spectators it was used for chariot races in the Byzantine age. It has now been restored and is used for a variety of different events. Thelmessos was also famous for its oracle in ancient times. The

Boats depart for the 'Blue Voyage' from the marina in Fethiye

FETHIYE

MAP INSIDE BACK COVER
(126 A4) *(ﬆ F6)* **Fethiye (population 60,000) is the largest town on the southwest coast and, even today, is not completely dominated by tourism.**
There is also a great deal of activity in the off-season as it is the most important market town for regional produce in the area. Fethiye was originally a Lycian town that was renamed Thelmessos after being conquered by Alexander the Great. An amphitheatre from this period has been

beautiful acropolis with a theatre, as well as the ruins of a fortress on the hill to the south of the town that was probably built by the Knights of St John of Jerusalem and later used by the Ottomans, can be visited.
The ★ *rock tombs* on the mountain slope to the south of the town centre conjure up a picture of Fethiye's Lycian origins. The most beautiful sarcophaguses can be seen next to the administration building at the port. Under the Ottomans, this important port was known as Megri. It was renamed again in 1934 in honour of the first Turkish pilot ever to be killed in battle,

Fethi Bey. The *Old Mosque (Eski Camii)* and ● *hamam* from the 18th century can be visited at the *market (paspatur)*. The beautiful bath with its 14 domes is still in operation and you should really try it out! Fethiye is a departure point for the famous 'Blue Voyages' and the Lycian Way *(see: Where to go)* and is perfectly located for trips to the surrounding countryside – on foot, by car or by boat. The bays between Fethiye and Göcek are especially popular with day-trippers: the comparatively large *Katrancı Bay*, where mixed woodland reaches down to the coastline, is 17 km (10½mi) away. Camping is permitted here from May to October. Further along the coast, you come to the more tranquil *Kızlar Bay*, also surrounded by pine trees and with several places to eat. A couple of miles from Katrancı – accessible either on foot or by bus – is *Günlüklü Bay* with its liquidambar trees, where you can also pitch your tent. *Küçük Kargi* is full of these trees and lies on the route the minibuses take back to Fethiye.

SIGHTSEEING

FETHIYE MÜZESI
The city museum has fine archaeological and ethnological departments with interesting finds dating back to the 8th century BC. *Tue–Sun 9am–5pm | entrance fee 5 lira | Kesikkapi Mah. Okul Sok. 1*

TOMB OF AMYNTAS 🔅
The most impressive Lycian royal tomb is high above the city (up 220 steps!). A carved stone portal lies behind the imposing 15 m (49 ft) high Ionian temple façade. The Lycians buried their dead in elevated rock chambers because they believed that the sirens would carry the souls of the deceased to heaven. Signposts show the way to the king's tomb. *Entrance fee 5 lira*

FOOD & DRINK

MEGRI LOKANTASI
An old restaurant at the market; excellent Turkish casseroles. *Çarşı Cad. 13 | tel. 0252 6 14 40 47 | Budget*

SPINNAKER
Chic fish restaurant on the promenade in Fethiye. *Kordon Boyu | tel. 0252 6 12 04 32 | Expensive*

SHOPPING

There is a traditional bazaar district *(paspatur)* in the centre of Fethiye where you can buy beautiful material, carpets, meerschaum pipes and sweets. The kilims are woven in the mountain villages and finished with natural root dyes. The narrow colourful cloth belts called *kolan* are typical of the region. The *weekly market*

THE SOUTHWEST COAST

(pazar) is held on Tuesdays and you will find everything – and even more – there. The *Imagine Bookstore (Cumhuriyet Cad. 9)* has a good selection of foreign-language books, maps and CDs.

BEACHES

Fethiye's beaches are located to the north of the town on the way to Göcek and, naturally, in Ölüdeniz. The largest – it is narrow but 5 km (3 mi) long – and most popular is *Çalış* and is particular good for surfing. If you are looking for something a little more peaceful, go to *Belcekız*, *Katrancı* or *Günlüklü*. Minibuses leave from the bus station in Fethiye.

LEISURE & SPORTS

The *European Diving Center (Kordon Cad. Hukuk Sitesi 20 | tel. 0252 6 14 97 71 | www. europeandiving.cu.uk)* or *Divers' Delight (Atatürk Cad. 38 | tel. 0252 6 12 10 99 | www.diversdelight.com)* cater to all divers' needs. Paragliding from 2000 m (6500 ft) high Babadağ down to Belcekız Beach is one of the most popular attractions *(Easy Riders | tel. 0252 6 17 01 48 | www.easy riderstravel.8m.com; Focus Team | tel. 0252 6 17 04 01 | www.focusparagliding. com; ExtremeTandem | tel. 0252 6 17 01 20 | around 240 lira)*. *Hotel Cypriot (25 rooms | Hisarönü | tel. 0252 6 16 79 16 | www.hotelcypriot.com)* and *Garfield Travel Agency (Fevzi Çakmak Cad. | Yat Limanı 9/B | tel. 0252 6 14 93 12 | 50–200 lira)* organise jeep safaris into the mountains. INSIDER TIP Microlight flights from Babadağ are all the rage: the light planes are motorised, the flight lasts about 22 minutes (around 220 lira). The pilot sits in the front and you take off from the airstrip in Ovacık near Hisarönü. Especially

So many things to buy at the weekly market in Fethiye

FETHIYE

popular: INSIDER TIP white water rafting on the River Dalaman, a 90 minute drive from Fethiye *(Activities Unlimited | PTT Karşısı | Hisarönü | tel. 0252 6 16 63 16 | www.activities-unlimited-turkey.com)*. And finally, Fethiye is a departure point for the ★ ● *'Blue Voyages'.* You can get information and take a look at the boats at the port; e.g. those from Kayhan Selçuk *(Alesta Yachting | Yat Limanı Karşısı | telgraf Apt. 9 | tel. 0252 6 14 18 61 | www.alesta yachting.com)*. Prices vary depending on the season, boat and route.

ENTERTAINMENT

There are many cafés and bars near the Old Bazaar and on the promenade at the port in Fethiye where you can sit for hours in the evening. The bars with the best atmosphere are in Ölüdeniz, on Belcekız Beach or at the lagoon itself. Minibuses travel back to Fethiye until midnight.

INSIDER TIP **BUZZ BAR**

Quiet bar under the roof of Deniz Camping directly on the sea; ideal for an aperitif at sunset. *Daily 9am–2am | Ölüdeniz | tel. 0252 6 17 05 26 | www.buzzbeachbar.com*

THE WHITE DOLPHIN BAR

Sophisticated terrace bar with candlelight, bougainvilleas and the magnificent starry sky overhead. *Daily 6pm–2am | Ölüdeniz | tel. 0252 6 16 60 36*

WHERE TO STAY

CLUB HOTEL LETOONIA

One of the most beautiful club complexes on the southwest coast, with a private beach 2 km (1¼ mi) long, is only 4 km (2½ mi) from Fethiye. The more than 40-acre property is located on a wooded promontory and has an indoor thalassic pool, sauna, sports facilities (tennis lessons also available) and several restau-

The thrill of rafting on the Dalaman

rants. *111 rooms, 509 bungalows | tel. 0242 4 44 02 80 | www.letoonia.com | Expensive*

INSIDER TIP ► FERAH PENSION

This guesthouse is also known as *Monica's Place*. It is only a 7-minute walk from the port and the rooms are clean, functional and bright. There is a wonderful panoramic view over Fethiye from the beds in the dormitory on the top floor. Beautiful inner courtyard for relaxing. *9 rooms plus dormitory | 2. Karagözler | Ordu cad. | tel. 0252 6 14 28 16 | www.ferahpension.com | Budget*

INSIDER TIP ► HILLSIDE BEACH CLUB

Exclusively located in a private bay; stylish family holidays with a wide range of sporting activities. The concept of the club is twofold: an active holiday with a lot of sport or a relaxing one with a 'silent beach'. Films evenings are held on the beach (no children allowed). Spacious rooms (215–540 ft²). *330 rooms | Kamelaya Koyu | tel. 0212 3 62 30 30 or 0252 614 83 60 | www.hillsidebeachclub.com.tr | Expensive*

OCAKKÖY

The former Greek village of Ovacik on the way to Ölüdeniz has become a dream in green: bungalows built of natural stone, extensive grounds, two pools. *8 rooms, 6 flats, 32 bungalows | Ovacık 7 km (4½ mi) from Fethiye | Ramazan Kaya | tel. 0252 6 16 61 56 (-57) | www.ocak-koy.com/index-eng.html | Moderate*

YACHT PLAZA HOTEL

This designer hotel opposite the marina is a good choice if you want to stay in Fethiye itself. Agreeably large rooms, good view and pool. *45 rooms | 1. Karagözler | tel. 0252 6 14 15 30 | www.yachthotelturkey.com | Moderate*

TURIZM DANIŞMA
Iskele Meydani 1 | tel. 0252 6 14 15 27 | www.fethiye.net

WHERE TO GO

GÖCEK (125 F6) *(E6)*
This little town at the northern end of Fethiye Gulf has now become one of the top addresses on the coast. It remained untouched until shortly after the turn of the millennium when a building boom started that has led to it becoming somewhat urbanised. Everything is focussed on the three marinas. Tours to the nearby bays and small islands depart from the harbour. These include tours to the seven *Yassıcalar Islands* ('The Flat Islands') that are reached after a 90-minute cruise and can be swum to after the anchor has been dropped. *Bedri Rahmi Koyu* is a bay named after the painter and poet Bedri Rahmi Eyüboglu (1911–75) – one of the intellectuals from Istanbul who cared more for Anatolian cultures than Islam. He immortalised himself with a painting of a fish on a rock here. Prices in Göcek are considerably higher than in other places. This also applies to the best hotel, the *Swissôtel Martina & Spa Resort* where you can drive to the beach in a golf buggy *(57 rooms | May–Oct | Cumhuriyet Mah. | tel. 0252 6 45 27 60 | goecek.swissotel.com | Expensive)*. The *Lykia Resort Hotel (95 rooms | tel. 0252 6 45 28 28 | www.goeceklykiaresort.com | Expensive)* is another very distinguished address. Göcek is also well suited for a relaxing holiday in a private rented flat; for example in the *Mr. Dim Apart Otel* with its outdoor pool *(13 rooms | Cumhuriyet Mah., İnönü Bulvar 1. Sok. | tel. 0252 6 45 19 69 | www.mrdim.com | Moderate)*. The best fish restaurant belongs to *Aliço (Göcek Yalısı | tel. 0252*

Deserted slopes: Kayaköy, the abandoned town

6 45 10 24 | *Moderate*). *Can* is less expensive but also very good *(tel. 0252 6 45 14 07 | Moderate)*. Those who want to have an especially elegant evening out should go to *North Shields Pub (Port Göcek)* later at night. *Around 30 km (18½mi) from Fethiye | minibuses from the bus station.*

KAYAKÖY ● (126 A5) (*Ø F6*)

Kayaköy (or Karmylassos) is an impressive monument to human irrationality. The village with two churches has a lovely location on a slope but, when you look more closely, you can see that most of the buildings have been abandoned. Kayaköy, which was formerly called Levisi, has been a ghost town since 1923. Until that time 3500 Greeks lived here. They had to leave their homes during the reciprocal population exchange agreement made after the Turkish victory in the War of Independence. Tourism, however, has now started to bring back some life. Restaurants, guesthouses and tea houses have been opened and the main church

is being restored. The INSIDER TIP *Kayo Sanat Kampı (Art Camp | tel. 0533 7 63 67 73 | www.sanatkampi.com)*, an artists initiative project, makes it possible for visitors to stay in restored houses and learn how to paint, photograph or make pottery while they are there *(Gençtur İstanbul | İstiklal Cad. 212 | Aznavur Pasajı Kat 5 Galatasaray | Beyoğlu | İstanbul tel. 0212 2 44 62 30 | www.genctur.com) Entrance fee 6 lira | 8 km (5 mi) from Fethiye | taxis only*

INSIDER TIP KELEBEKLER VADISI (BUTTERFLY VALLEY) (126 A5) (*Ø F7*)

The valley in Faralya, 5 km (3 mi) south of Ölüdeniz, is a small piece of heaven on earth. It cuts deep into the mountains and ends at a wonderful beach. In ancient times it was known as Perdicia but the people living there renamed it Güldürümsü in the 19th century. The isolated canyon is surrounded by rock walls up to 400 m (1300 ft) high and a waterfall plummets almost 60 m (200 ft) at the upper end. As there is little accommodation here except for a few bungalows, camping is a good alternative; showers and WCs do exist but you don't expect much from the sanitary installations *(tel. 0555 6 32 02 37)*. The valley is famous for its rare butterflies and as a place to watch shooting stars especially from mid-July to the end of August. There is a relatively frequent minibus service from the bus station. The trail from the village of Faralya to the valley is quite a difficult hike. One path starts near the *George House Pension (12 bungalows and tents to rent | Kelebekler Vadisi Girişi | tel. 0252 6 42 11 02)*; sections of it are very precipitous and walkers may need to hang on to the fixed ropes there. The descent takes about 45 minutes and can only be recommended for those with no fear of heights. The most comfortable alternative is to take the boat from Belcikiz beach in Ölüdeniz. *(June–Sept departures daily 11am, noon, 2pm, 4pm, 6pm and 7pm; return to Ölüdeniz 9.30am, 10.30am, 1pm, 2.30pm, 5pm and 6pm; from there, the way back to Fethiye is easy)*.

ÖLÜDENIZ ★ ●
(126 A5) *(🕮 F6–7)*

The lagoon that is only connected to the sea by a narrow outlet is a real eye-catcher: sky-blue water and beaches of white sand framed by a pine forest: the perfect idyll! A 14 km (8½ mi) serpentine road through the mountains links Fethiye with *Belcekız Beach*, the left section of the large bay with the *Ölüdeniz Lagoon* at its right end. 2300 acres of land here have been declared a nature reserve. Thirty years ago Ölüdeniz was an insiders' tip where globetrotters on their way to Kathmandu liked to make a stopover. Today, the Ölüdeniz section is a public beach which you have to pay to use. Canoes and kayaks are available for hire. There are still places to camp at Belcekız Beach but this paradise is not nearly as isolated as it used to be. However, INSIDER TIP *Hotel Meri*, the oldest hotel in the area, *(94 rooms | tel. 0252 6 17 00 01 | www.hotelmeri.com | Moderate)* has remained a quiet place – especially in spring and autumn. The bars at Belcekız Beach are the most beautiful in the Fethiye region. *12 km (7½ mi) from Fethiye | minibuses from the bus station*

PINARA (126 A5) *(🕮 F7)*

It is well worth making the trip from Fethiye to the remains of the ancient Lycian city of Pinara for its magnificent location alone. It lies on a high plateau that drops down steeply on three sides and ends at a rock wall with tombs hewn into it. There is a magnificent panoramic view as well as impressive testimonies to an ancient culture from around 400 BC. The distance from the city gate to the royal tombs and the ruins of a theatre and fortress will give you an idea of the approximate size this city once had. *Entrance fee 6 lira | 40 km (25 mi) from Fethiye towards Kalkan*

TWELVE ISLAND TOUR
(125 F6) *(🕮 E–F6)*

You set sail from the quay in the morning: the excursion boats depart for *Oniki Adala Turu* between 10am–11am. Ölüdeniz and the islands near Göcek lie on the route. The larger islands are *Kızılada* (Red Island), *Delkili* (Hole Island), *Yassıca* (The Flat Island), *Tersane* (Shipyard Island), *Domuz* (Pig Island) and *Şövalye* (Knights' Island). The latter was used by crusaders from Rhodes and is still inhabited today. The remains of an old shipyard can be visited on Tersane and you can see the ruins of a Byzantine monastery below the water in what is called Hamam Bay where boats stop for a swimming break. You will also have the possibility to explore further inland while the boats lie at anchor.

MARMARIS

▓▓▓ **MAP INSIDE BACK COVER**
▓▓▓ (125 D5) (*🗺 D6*) **Marmaris is one of those towns that insiders become wistful about when they tell of how idyllic it was 20 years ago.**
And actually, hardly anything remains today on the large, almost closed, fjord-like bay, of the picturesque port of Physkos that was part of the Carian Empire in the 6th century BC. Even more than Bodrum and Fethiye, Marmaris (pop. more than 120,000 in summer) has become a purely tourist resort. Every year the slope outside the town, from where visitors have a spectacular view over Marmaris and the bay, becomes increasingly disfigured by advertising boards for hotels, restaurants and bars. There are currently 50,000 beds for tourists in the greater Marmaris area. The entire bay is built up with one hotel next to another, and the 1500 moorings at *Netsel Marina* make it the largest base for sailing boats and yachts in the entire eastern Mediterranean. The result is that, despite its perfectly developed tourist infrastructure, Marmaris can be loud and overcrowded in the high season. If you just want to spend a holiday by the seaside, you should look for accommodations in *Turunç* or *İcmerler*, a little bit out of town, where it is more peaceful and the water cleaner.
The cultural side of things in Marmaris has improved too: the amphitheatre seats 7000 and there are often **INSIDER TIP** open-air concerts in the historical fortress; the MAKSAD Culture and Art Society and the chamber orchestra have made the tourism metropolis famous far beyond its borders (tickets: *biletix.com.tr*). A municipal Academy of Art and the cultural centre have turned Marmaris into a genuine artistic city that shows itself from its best side in spring and autumn. Excursion boats leave for surrounding beaches from in front of the Atatürk Monument on Yeni Kordon every morning at around 10am *(12–25 lira)*. Longer tours to Ekincik, Dalyan or Bodrum depart from the port and daily ferries to Rhodes sail from behind the yacht marina *(www.marmaris-travel.com)*.

SIGHTSEEING

KALE (CASTLE)
Suleiman the Magnificent built this castle on the site of an Ionian fortress in 1522 as a base for his Rhodes campaigns. There is a small museum *(Tue–Sun 8am–noon, 1pm–3pm)* with archaeological and folkloric exhibits in the castle that towers prominently over the port *(entrance 5 lira)*. The *Hafza Sultan caravanserai* in the centre of town, where there is one souvenir shop after the next, was also erected in the 16th century.

FOOD & DRINK

There are some fairly good *lokanta* and doner kebab kiosks in and near the bazaar. British breakfast is very popular in Marmaris. In the evening, most people promenade around the old port where most of the restaurants have fixed-price meals.

BEDESTEN
An oasis in the midst of all the hustle and bustle: simple, but very popular tea house with hookahs in historical surroundings near the mosque. *Çeşme Meydanı | Budget*

BUHARA
With its good food, large selection and reasonable prices, the Buhara stands out from many of the other restaurants. *Marina | tel. 0252 412 39 69 | Moderate*

A lovely place for dinner: restaurant terrace above the port in Marmaris

INSIDER TIP ▶ DEDE RESTAURANT

Specialises in fish and seafood: the fish casserole is particularly recommendable. *Barbaros Cad. | tel. 0252 413 12 52 | www. dederestaurant.com | Moderate*

MY MARINA ENGLISH PUB

This British pub is one of the best in town. They have other kinds of beer as well as ale! *Netsel Marina | tel. 0252 413 04 31 | Expensive*

SOFRA

Enormous choice of starters, kebab, *pide* and home-style cooking. Open from early in the morning to late at night. This is where the locals come to eat. *36. Sokak | Budget*

SHOPPING

The boutiques at *Netsel Marina* are the most expensive places to shop; the weekly market is the cheapest. *Marmari merkezi* is the name of the bazaar with hundreds of leather, carpet and jewellery shops whose owners have become somewhat spoiled by tourists from cruise ships. The less expensive jewellers are in *Çarşi*. Many people like to have shoes made to measure in Marmaris. The market is held in a multi-storey car park in the new city on Friday and many farmers from neighbouring villages come and sell their fresh produce.

BEACHES

Marmaris has a sandy beach that seems to be squeezed between the sea and the promenade along the shore and which is usually overcrowded. It is better to take a boat to *Cennet Island*, or to Amazon and Kilise Bay. The boats set sail from in front of the Atatürk Monument at the port.

ENTERTAINMENT

● *Hacı Mustafa Sokak* is Marmaris' lively nightlife street. This is where you will find numerous bars that are also perfect for a drink in the early evening. The *Marina* is expensive but has a wonderful view over the bay. There are lovely beach bars on *Uzun Yalı Sokak*. The moonlight boat trip is an unforgettable experience – the boats are floating bars. *(10pm–around 2am |*

12.50 lira | departure from the port). The *Netsel Marina Cinema* shows the latest international blockbusters in their original language (mostly English) with Turkish subtitles *(Yat Limanı | tel. 0252 4 12 27 08)*.

BAR X

Bar X, with a terrace bar, beach bar and 2700 ft² indoor disco, is one of the most popular places to spend a long night in Marmaris. *Daily to 4am | Uzun Yalı Sok. 72| tel. 0252 4 13 13 45*

CHEERS DANCE BAR

Cocktail bar that gradually turns into a disco as the night progresses. The music from the 1960s and '70s not only attracts the young crowd. *Daily 7pm–4am | behind the Shell petrol station, near the coast | tel. 0252 4 12 67 22*

GREEN HOUSE

One of the most popular locations in Marmaris' pub district. Also open in winter. *Hacı Mustafa Sok. 89 | tel. 0252 4 12 50 71*

WHERE TO STAY

ANEMON

Centrally-located, well-managed, medium standard hotel with a swimming pool. Also open in winter. This is the right place to stay if you don't need to be on the bay. *89 rooms | Kemal Elgin Bulvari 63 | tel. 0252 4 13 30 31 | www.anemonhotels.com/marmaris.asp | Budget*

GÜLSAH PANSIYON

Set back from the main road, this charming guesthouse has been an institution in Marmaris for 40 years. The sandy beach is only a stone's throw away. There is a café in front of the building where you can have breakfast or drink a beer in the evening. The rooms are air-conditioned and have small balconies. *20 rooms | Atatürk Cad. 52 | tel. 0252 4 12 66 42 | www.gulsahpansiyon.com | Budget*

IRMAK APART HOTEL

This hotel with a swimming pool and cheerful, spotless rooms and flats is a little more than 1000 m from the centre of town and just 200 m from the nearest supermarket and beach. The outside pool is small but adequate. *38 rooms, 25 flats | Siteler Mah., 187 Sok. 5 | tel. 0252 4 12 43 86 | hotelirmak.com | Budget–Moderate*

PUPA YACHT HOTEL

This friendly hotel a bit away from the centre is owned by the Pupa charter agency that also organises 'Blue Voyages'. *19 rooms | Addagzi | tel. 0252 4 13 35 66 | www.pupa.com.tr | Moderate*

INFORMATION

TURIZM DANIŞMA

Iskele Meydanı 2 | tel. 0252 4 12 10 35 | www.marmaris-online.com | www.marmaris info.com

WHERE TO GO

REŞADIYE PENINSULA
(124 A–C 5–6) *(ᗰ A–C6)*

The Reşadiye Peninsula, shaped like a finger and thumb, juts out into the Aegean to the west of Marmaris. Ancient *Knidos* and the tranquil port of *Bozburun* at the two ends are popular destinations for yachtsmen. This largely untouched environment is dominated by three natural products: honey, olives and almonds. 52 bays can be found around the peninsula; the most famous are *Palamatbükü, Hayitbükü* and *Ovabükü*. The old centre of *Datça (Eski Datça)* is in the middle of the peninsula. Turkish intellectuals and artists have set up home here in expensively restored stone houses. The new city is further to the west, near the sea. Many plant-lovers visit Datça as 849 plant species can be found here, 25 of which are endemic. More detailed information is available from the *Datça Tourism Association DAÇEV (Atatürk Cad. 71, Sok. 1 | www.dacev.org.tr)*. The ● *Badem Motel* is a pleasant, family-run business in crystal-clear Palamatbükü Bay; it is a pleasant surprise to find that such simple, clean places to stay, which also serve good food, still exist on the shores of the Mediterranean *(16 rooms | Palamatbükü Sahili | tel. 0252 725 51 83 | www. bademotel.com | Budget)*.

INSIDER TIP *Bozburun* is still considered a refuge for dropouts disenchanted with modern civilisation. Nevertheless everything can be found there: a small marina, restaurants and cafés along the harbour wall, a few small guesthouses and very little traffic as the road ends in Bozburun. The small town is famous for its boatyards. This is where many of the *gulets* are built – the large wooden sailing boats that you can take from Marmaris or Bodrum on a 'Blue Voyage'. *Sabrinas Haus* on the shore is a luxurious place to stay *(20 rooms | tel.*

0252 4 56 20 45 | www.sabrinashaus.com | Expensive).

TURUNÇ
(125 D5) (𝄞 C–D 6)

Only a few years ago, Turunç was still a well-kept secret. Today it is a destination for minibus tours from Marmaris (about 20 km/12 mi away) and has experienced a tourist boom as a result. In spite of this, the bay surrounded by high mountains is still a wonderful place for families to spend their holiday with small pensions and only a short walk to the beach. *Adrienne's House* on the outskirts of the village is a good address: It is run by an English couple, serves an English breakfast and has a lovely pool *(5 rooms | Gülhak Mah 41. | tel. 0252 4 76 79 51 | Moderate)*. The ⚘ INSIDER TIP *Loryma Resort Hotel* is an alternative: It is a sophisticated, ecologically friendly apartment hotel high above Turunç with spectacular views, magnificent pool, home-made food, child-care service and a shuttle bus to the beach *(80 flats | tel. 0252 4 76 72 20 | www.loryma.com | Expensive)*.

Building a traditional *gulet* in Bozburun

ANTALYA – LYCIAN COAST

The coast of ancient Lycia stretches from Fethiye to Antalya. The mountains force their way into the sea. The steep slopes of the Taurus only a narrow strip of rugged coastline in many places. The contrast between the flanks of the mountain that remain green throughout the year and the deep blue sea is what makes this section of the coast so special.

In some places the road is no more than a shelf cut into the hillside with a plunging drop to the sea on one side and the sheer side of the mountain rising up on the other. When it became too narrow, the cost road was moved inland where it is well-developed and relative easy to drive.

The Lycian Coast is a destination for tourists looking for something special and not just a beach holiday. The historical centres of old Lycia are located just beyond Fethiye towards Antalya. Visitors can make tours of ancient holy sites, dive down to sunken cities off the coast and admire the eternal flames on Mount Olympos at night. Beach holiday-makers will also find their dream hotel here. Holiday resorts, which are among the best in all of Turkey, have been established on the last 100 km (62 mi) before Antalya around the former fishing village of Kemer. Sun, sea and fun attract millions of holiday-makers every year. And with its secluded fishing villages and small

Photo: View over the Old Town of Antalya

Bays, mountains, impressive rock tombs and Antalya, the lively metropolis on the south coast

places still untouched by tourism, the Lycian Coast is ideal for a romantic holiday.

ANTALYA

MAP INSIDE BACK COVER
(127 E–F3) (*Ø K5–6*) **Antalya** (pop. metropolitan area: 1.9 million) is much more than just the largest hub and

CITY WHERE TO START?
Saat Kulesi: The centre is the square with the clock tower beneath the 'fluted minaret'. From here, you can stroll down to the streets of the Old Town or to the nearby bazaar. Buses and shared taxis leave for the beaches from the clock tower.

ANTALYA

commercial centre on the south coast. It is one of the most beautiful cities in Turkey and an economic boomtown.

Despite this, its heart is still intact. The Old Town, the *Kaleiçi* (lit. 'inner fortress'), is a real gem. It has one of the largest ensembles of wooden Ottoman houses to be found in Turkey. The historical Old Town is enclosed by a wall and the most famous entrance to the *Kaleiçi* is through the almost 2000-year-old Hadrian's Gate built to celebrate the visit by the Roman emperor around 160 AD.

The second landmark of the city, the *Yivli Minare* ('fluted minaret'), a tower erected in 1220 in honour of the Seljuk ruler İzzedin Keyhüsrev who liberated the city from the Byzantines, is also in the Old Town. The *Ulu Camii*, a mosque built in 1373 that is impressive through its simplicity, stands next to the tower. The *clock tower* above the minaret, another landmark, is an expression of the modern 19th-century city. *Uzun Çarşi Sokak,* one of the main streets, leads through the Old Town, past souvenir shops, to the harbour. *Cumhuriyet Caddesi*, a promenade lined with palm trees, starts to the right of the clock tower (looking towards the Old Town) and forms the western boundary of the old city. There are many lovely tea gardens and small parks from where you have a fantastic view of the *Kaleiçi* and the harbour along the promenade. There are also several restaurants here that are well worth visiting in the evening, if only for the view.

Antalya's bazaar begins opposite the clock tower as does a pedestrian precinct with many inexpensive restaurants offering good food in the side streets. *Atatürk Caddesi* also starts at the clock tower and runs to the east along the city wall to the large main park that ends at the steep cliffs by the sea. Atatürk Caddesi is Antalya's main shopping street where you can find everything from expensive boutiques to second-hand fashion.

A top address – Alp Paşa Konaği restaurant

SIGHTSEEING

ANTALYA MÜZESI (ARCHAEOLOGICAL MUSEUM) ★ ●

The Archaeological Museum in Antalya is one of the most important in Turkey. In addition to prehistoric finds, including those from nearby Karain Cave, the museum dazzles visitors with original statues from the ancient town of Perge as well as gold and silver jewellery, weapons and clothes. *Cumhuriyet Cad., corner Konyaaltı Cad. | Tue–Sun 9am–12.30pm, 1.30pm–5pm | entrance fee 25 lira*

KALEIÇI (OLD TOWN) ★ ●

As soon as you leave the modern metropolis and enter the maze of small streets you will feel as if you have stepped back in time. The labyrinthine lanes are often so narrow that cars cannot be driven here. Many of the former large city villas have been saved from ruin and have now been converted into charming small hotels. Even though, at first glance, this all seems to be very confusing, all of the paths lead down to the harbour. Pubs and restaurants rub shoulders to each other around the harbour; steep steps lead down to beer gardens with wonderful views of the ships. Not far from Hadrian's Gate at *Kocatepe Sokak 25*, INSIDER TIP *Kaleiçi Museum* has been established in one of the old mansions, the so-called *konaks*, where you can get an impression of how life was lived by a typical family in this district *(Thu–Tue 9am–6pm | entrance fee 7.50 lira)*.

FOOD & DRINK

INSIDER TIP ALP PAŞA KONAĞI

Enjoying specialities from the buffet, sitting around the pool of this lovely townhouse and listening to piano music is a really special experience. *Kaleiçi | Hesapçı Sok. | tel. 0242 2 47 56 76 | www.alppasa.com | Expensive*

EXTRABLATT

This branch of a German coffee-house chain serves German and Italian food in a bistro-like atmosphere. This is a meeting place for everyone in Antalya. *Alanya Karayolu 26 | Şirinyalı Mah. İsmet Gökşen Cad. 10, Lider Plaza | tel. 0242 3 16 60 07 | www.cafe-extrablatt.com | Moderate*

HACI HASAN

A little bit off the beaten track behind the bazaar, this restaurant is open during the day and serves good Turkish food. *Balbey Malhallesi | 444 Sokak 10 (near the Balbey Mosque) | tel. 0242 2 42 55 82 | Budget*

INSIDER TIP 7 MEHMET

He has a scar on his forehead that looks like a 7 and that is why he has been called '7 Mehmet' since his schooldays. Mehmet started as a soup cook in the bazaar but today he runs one of the best restau-

★ **Antalya Müzesi**
Archaeological Museum which includes statues from Perge → p. 52

★ **Kaleiçi (Old Town)**
The beautiful Ottoman Old Town with its lanes, restaurants and shops frames Antalya's port → p. 52

★ **Perge**
Ancient harbour town with market street and large stadium → p. 57

★ **Termessos**
Unconquerable Lycian mountain fortress with a theatre at an altitude of 1000 m → p. 58

★ **Patara**
A Roman harbour city lies buried under the beautiful beach → p. 60

★ **Xanthos**
A visit to the main city of the former Lycian realm near Kınık → p. 61

★ **Kekova**
A sunken city in the crystal-clear water of the bay at Kekova → p. 65

★ **Myra**
Magnificent Lycian rock tombs in the town St Nicholas came from → p. 66

★ **Phaselis**
Ancient harbour city with a fine beach, ancient theatre and pine forest near Kemer → p. 69

rants in Antalya with a magnificent view and superb Turkish-Ottoman cooking. *Atatürk Kültür Park 201 | tel. 0242 2 38 52 00 | www.7mehmet.com | Moderate–Expensive*

SHOPPING

You will find textiles, leather, jewellery and souvenirs – everything your heart could desire – in the 128 shops under the roof of the gigantic ● *Migros* Shopping Centre *(www.antalyamigros.com)* in the district of the same name. *Konyaaltı* is Antalya's more traditional shopping district. There are many small souvenir shops and carpet dealers in the *Kaleiçi*. Weekly markets: between *Ali Çetinkay* and *Mevlana Cad. (Tue)*, *Isıklar Cad. (Wed)*, around *Konyaaltı (Fri)* and in *Lara (Sat)*. *Döşemealtı* (pronounced 'dershme'alti') nomad carpets are a speciality of Antalya. The most inexpensive place to buy these hand-woven carpets coloured with natural dyes is in the village of INSIDER TIP *Kovanlik (35 km/22 mi, minibus from bus station)*.

BAZAAR 54

A large shopping centre for tourists: carpets, jewellery, leatherwear; good quality, not overpriced. A bit out of town in Serik. *Aspendos Bulvarı, Demokrasi Kavşaği | Serik | www.bazaar54.net*

DERIMOD

The best Turkish label for leather clothing is not very expensive; in the Migros Shopping Centre. *Migros Alışveriş Merkezi | B 11–12 | Migros*

GÜVEN

Gold and silver jewellery is less expensive in Antalya than in tourist centres such as Kemer, Side or Alanya. There are many jewellers, including Güven, at the north end of Atatürk Avenue. The day's gold price is displayed in shop windows *Atatürk Cad. 25*

NETWORK/ALTINYILDIZ

The chain of clothing for men and women is notable for excellent material and classical design. *Konyaaltı Cad. 24/2*

INSIDER TIP PAŞABAHÇE

The state-run glass and porcelain factory offers high quality at low prices. Everyday crockery, high-quality china, modern glass design, imported goods as well as expensive copies of old Ottoman pieces. The goods are expertly packed for shipment *In the Carrefour Shopping Centre, Şirinyal Mah., İsmet Gökşen Cad. (opposite Lider Plaza)*

BEACHES

There are two beaches close to Antalya; *Lara* and *Konyaaltı*. Buses depart from Atatürk Avenue for Lara with its fine sand 10 km (6 mi) away. In recent years, this has developed into a new hotel district where so-called theme hotels such as the 'Titanic', 'Kremlin' and 'The White House' are particularly dominant. Konyaaltı beach lies to the west between the cliffs with the Beydağları Mountains in the background. Entrance to the beach is free; a charge is made for umbrellas and sunbeds. Buses leave from near the Archaeological Museum. Please note: the water gets deep very quickly here! Boats set sail for the beaches from the Old Town in the morning. Small *Mermeli* beach lies directly in the Old Town; however, it is a better idea to take the boat across to *Sıçan Island*.

LEISURE & SPORTS

Tours to all the sights and destinations are offered by operators in Antalya. These in clude jeep safaris to the Taurus Mountains and rafting on the River Köprüçay. There

a session with peeling and massage costs around 30 lira).

A stroll around the many shops in the streets of the Old Town is a must

are even helicopter tours to Pamukkale and Cappadocia – it is only a question of price *(e.g. Maki Tour | Kaleiçi | Uzun Çarşı Sok. 16/B | tel. 0242 2 41 45 41).*
The *Rainbow Diving School* is located in the port; it offers courses and excursions for experienced divers. Diving to a shipwreck near the coast or exploring underwater caves is a fascinating experience. *(Kaleiçi | Yat Limani 30 | tel. 0242 2 48 12 57 | www. apdivers.de/en).* There is a ● **INSIDER TIP** historical *hamam* from the 15th century in the centre of the Old Town. The Turkish bath has been carefully restored and offers all services: separate steam baths and massages for men and women *(daily 9am–11pm | Sefa Hamamı | Kaleiçi | Barbaros Mah., Kocatepe Sok. 32 | tel. 0242 2 41 23 21 | www.sefahamam.com |*

ENTERTAINMENT

Antalya combines the advantages of a large city with the facilities of a tourist centre. There are several theatres and cinemas (e.g. in the Migros Shopping Centre). The renowned film festival *Altın Portakal* ('Golden Orange' *www.altin portakal.org.tr*) is held at the end of September every year. In addition to the pubs at the port, there are also three large discos; the best is *Club 29* with an open-air dance floor. The *Olympus Disco* in the garden of the Falez Hotel on Konyyaltı beach and the fashionable *Jolly Joker* with retro-music from the 1980s and Turkish rock *(İsmet Gökşen Cad. | opposite Carrefour Shopping Centre, Lara)* are also very popular.

Romantic: night time panorama of Antalya's port

WHERE TO STAY

HILLSIDE SU ●

Exquisite five-star hotel with a private beach, spa centre and various sporting offers. Minimalist design, white rooms, expensive materials. Not suitable for children. *294 rooms, 41 suites | Konyaaltı | tel. 0242 2 49 07 00 | www.hillsidesu.com | Expensive*

KALEICI PANSIYON

Attractive little guesthouse right in the centre making it easy to reach all the sights. Air-conditioning, lovely garden with pool. *10 rooms | Kılıçaslan Mah., Sakarya Sok. 11 | tel. 0242 2 44 71 46 | www.kaleicipansiyon. com | Budget*

TEKELI KONAKLARI

Beautiful boutique hotel in the Old Town. Six lovingly restored Ottoman townhouses: everything is handmade – from the tiles to the cedar-wood ceilings. *8 rooms | Dizdar Hasan Sokak | tel. 0242 2 44 54 65 | www.tekeli.com.tr | Moderate*

TUNALI APART

Simple, spotless holiday flats for 4 (pullout sofa for 2 additional guests) with TV and air-conditioning. There is a pool, restaurant and pool bar in the garden and the beach is only 250 m away. *16 flats | Akdeniz Bulvarı, Liman Mah., 5. Sok. 2 | tel. 0242 2 59 07 00 | www.tunaliapart. com | Moderate*

VILLA PERLA

Magnificently restored villa in the old town: glazed terrace, pool, garden. There is a Byzantine cistern under the house; the rooms are comfortable and spacious. INSIDER TIP First-class restaurant. *10 rooms | Barbaros Mah., Hesapçi Sok. 26 | tel. 0242 2 48 97 93 | www.villaperla.com | Expensive*

INFORMATION

TURIZM DANIŞMA
*Cumhuriyet Caddesi | Özel İdarfe İşhani |
tel. 0242 2 41 17 47 | www.antalya-ws.com*

WHERE TO GO

DÜDEN WATERFALLS ●
(127 F3) (⊞ K5)

The River Düden forms two waterfalls in the immediate vicinity of Antalya and both are well worth visiting. The first is to the north-east of the city centre where the river emerges from the Taurus Mountains. The second waterfall plummets over the steep cliffs directly into the sea. Although the lower waterfall *(Aşağı Düden Şelasi)*, 8 km (5 mi) from the centre of Antalya on the road towards Lara beach, is more spectacular – the water plummets 60 m into the sea – the upper waterfall also has its charm. A lovely park has been laid out around it that is the perfect place for a stroll. A flight of steps leads up to a cave behind the waterfall. However, in July and August the Düden is often only a mere trickle because its water is channelled off to irrigate the cotton fields. *The arterial road to the north (Düden Şelalesi junction) is signposted | minibuses from the bus station*

ELMALI (126 C4) (⊞ H6)

The extensive forests around Antalya have not only been decimated in modern times. For thousands of years, wood – in particular cedar *(Cedrus libani)* that is indispensible for the hulls of ships – has been a valuable commodity that all civilisations have ravaged. There are several dozen protected, more-than-1000-year old, trees in the *Elmalı Nature Reserve* including the 25 m (82 ft) high and 2015-year-old *Koca Katran* tree. The nature reserve lies in the mountains around 165 km (102 mi) from Antalya and 16 km (10 mi) from the small town of Elmalı. It is a good idea to hire a local guide to help you find the ancient trees. *(Serdar Çakar: tel. 0532 4 57 39; forest ranger: tel. 0242 6 18 25 01).* If you continue your hike in this magnificent stretch of countryside, overnight accommodation can be found in the village of Akçeniş (Hotel Three Angels | tel. 0242 6 25 50 59 | www.hotelucmelekler. com | *Moderate)*

PERGE ★
(127 F3) (⊞ K5)

Perge (18 km/11 mi east of Antalya) was one of the largest ancient Greek cities on the southern coast of Anatolia. A tour of the excavation site will give you an idea of just how large the settlement must have been. The remains of buildings from Antiquity lie scattered over an enormous area and are still waiting to be classified. A large section of the city has been well preserved. The *stadium*, on the road from the car park, is the best preserved in all Turkey. Gladiator fights were held here in Roman times. The former market, the *agora*, is very beautiful and you can still make out the outlines of the shops that used to line the main street. It is said that Bartholdi took the Artemis relief on one of the columns on the left side of the main avenue as his model for New York's Statue of Liberty – it was originally planned to place this at the entrance to the Suez Canal. The *khedive*, the Ottoman Sultan's governor in Egypt, Ismail Pascha was afraid of being accused of idolatry and refused to have the statue placed there. The artwork was stored in Paris for a while before finally being shipped to America in 350 individual sections and reconstructed there in 1885.

If possible, you should try to visit Perge when it is not too hot because there is very little shade on this large site. *Towards*

In the footsteps of the Greeks and Romans: the ruins at Perge

Alanya as far as Aksu and then 3 km (2 mi) along a small (signposted) road to Perge | minibuses from Antalya bus station | daily 8am–6pm | entrance fee 12.50 lira

TERMESSOS ★ ☆ (127 E3) (⏍ J5)

One of the most impressive ancient sites in Turkey lies high up in the Taurus Mountains to the north of Antalya: Termessos is located like an eagle's nest on a mountain slope at a height of more than 1000 m (3300 ft) in the middle of this range's magnificent scenery. It is the only Lycian city Alexander the Great never succeeded in conquering. Its unique location offered it protection from all besiegers. Sections of the former city wall have been preserved to this day as have the remains of temples and a theatre built on the mountain slope from where there is a wonderful view of the surrounding mountains and forests. However, it is still not easy to reach Termessos. The excavation site is in a national park and the shared taxis *(dolmuş)* from Antalya

only drive to the entrance where you can get your first information on the ancient city in the small museum. Children can look at stuffed animals and explore tree houses. If you are in your own car or taxi, you can continue the 9 km (5½ mi) along the steep road to a car park from where there is still a good 20-minute walk waiting for you. *35 km (22 mi) towards Korkuteli | in the Güllük-Daği National Park | daily 8am–6pm | entrance fee 7.50 lira*

KALKAN

(126 B6) (⏍ F7) A few years ago The Independent newspaper listed Kalkan among the best tourist destinations, especially for those seeking a romantic vacation.

Kalkan (pop. 4000) is small, exclusive, an architectural jewel and has long been a refuge for the Turkish upper class who find Bodrum, Marmaris and Antalya too overcrowded. Today, Kalkan has become very British. While Alanya is firmly in German hands, Kalkan is dominated by the English who have bought second homes here. Residents of this picturesque town have taken care to preserve its historical substance and to prevent ugly blocks of flats from being built. *Kaputaş Beach* nearby and the large sandy beach at *Patara* offer excellent conditions for swimming and sunbathing. Kalkan is a perfect centre from which to visit some of the most important Lycian sites such as *Xanthos* and *Letoon*.

FOOD & DRINK

CAFÉ DEL MAR

This family-run business is one of the most popular coffee houses in Kalkan. There are good cocktails, as well as homemade cakes and snacks such as toast and hamburgers. Free WLAN connection and book exchange. *Yalıboyu Mah., Hasan Altan Cad. 61 | tel. 0242 8 44 10 68 | www.cafedelmar kalkan.com | Budget*

INSIDER TIP PATLICAN (AUBERGINE)

The restaurant on the harbour wall has been run by Mehmet Bilgiç since 1996 and gourmets consider it to be one of the best on the southern coast. In addition to fish, there is also game and aubergine *güvec* – an exquisite vegetable casserole served in a clay pot. *Yalıboyu Mah. Mole 25–27 | tel. 0242 8 44 33 32 | www.kalkan aubergine.com | Expensive*

UÇ KARDEŞLER ALABALIK

A garden restaurant in the village of İslamlar, 10 km (6 mi) from Kalkan for those who like simple country food and freshly caught trout from its own ponds. The temperature in this mountain village is quite cool even at the height of summer. *İslamlar | tel. 0242 8 38 61 55 | Moderate*

BEACHES

There is a pebbly beach on the eastern outskirts of Kalkan itself. Kaputaş Plajı, 8 km (5 mi) away, is much nicer but it is small and soon becomes overcrowded. This makes a day trip by boat from the port in Kalkan even more attractive when you will be able to go swimming as well as visit caves and bizarre rock formations.

ENTERTAINMENT

In Kalkan, most people sit in restaurants until late at night. Many hotels have lovely terrace bars that holiday-makers try out one after the other. There are more at the port *(Yalı, Yachtpoint Bar, Fener Café)*, all on the Yalıboyu Promenade or on Iskele Sokak.

The beautiful beach near Kalkan: Kaputaş Plajı

WHERE TO STAY

CLUB XANTHOS HOTEL
The club hotel is directly on the beach in nearby Kalamar Bay. Large rooms. Seawater is used for the pool. *70 rooms, 9 suites | Kalmar Koyu | tel. 0252 8 44 23 88 | www.clubxanthos.com | Moderate*

KALKAN HAN
Unassuming, standard category hotel in the centre of Kalkan. Hospitable atmosphere, Turkish and international guests. *6 rooms, 4 suites | Köyiçi | tel. 0242 8 44 3151 | www.kalkan.org.tr | Moderate*

INSIDER TIP VILLA MAHAL
White-and-blue villa high above Kalkan; luxuriously furnished with a private beach, this is one of the most exclusive addresses in town. Expensive, but incredibly beautiful. *11 rooms, 2 suites | opposite Club Patara | tel. 0242 8 44 32 68 | www.villa mahal.com | Expensive*

WHERE TO GO

LETOON (KUMLOVA)
(126 A5–6) (*M* F7)
Letoon was the religious centre of the Greek Lycian League. This was the site of the important temple to the goddess Leto and her children Apollo and Artemis. The Lycians probably already had a place of worship here before they came under Greek influence after being conquered by Alexander the Great.

Unfortunately, only a few stumps of the columns of the so-called *Stoa Hall* in front of what was once the largest Leto Temple can still be seen. They look like the remains of a sunken temple because, over time, the groundwater has risen so much that the foundations of the hall have disappeared under the water. The remains of three other temples are located a little higher up: the *Sanctuary of Leto*, the former *Apollo Temple* with the small building in honour of *Artemis* between the two. The temples were built between 400 and 150BC. In addition to the temples, visitors to Letoon can find Roman and Byzantine buildings including a theatre and basilica. *Entrance fee 5 lira | turn off the road to Fethiye 2 km (1¼mi) after the village of Kınık, then 4 km (2½mi) to the sanctuary*

PATARA ★
(126 A6) (*M* F7)
Patara, at the mouth of the River Eşen (Xanthos), was one of the six important Lycian metropolises (Xanthos, Patara, Pinara, Tlos, Myra and Olympos) that each had three votes in the League. The Lycian 'parliament' was made up of 1400 representatives who met in Patara. Before it became silted up in the 9th century, the harbour city lay approximately 30 m higher than it does today. The excavation site is now around 600 m further inland. Apollo, the god of moral purity and moderation, prophecy and the arts, music, poetry and song is said to have spent his winters here on the endless beaches. The sanctuary at Delphi, the holiest oracle site of ancient times, was dedicated to him *(www.patara-excavations.com, www.lycian turkey.com)*.

Today, not much of the former glory remains. The *city gate* from 100AD and the *theatre* on the northern slope are the best-preserved remains. The harbour is completely silted up and the largest section of the city has disappeared beneath the sand. But this has turned what was once the largest harbour into the biggest and most beautiful beach (600 m wide, 19 km/12 mi long) on the entire Lycian coast. The small, peaceful INSIDER TIP *Patara View Point Hotel* on the magnificent sandy beach near the village of *Gelemiş* is a little piece of heaven on earth

(15 rooms, 6 villas with private pools | tel. 0252 8 43 51 84 | www.pataraviewpoint. com | Moderate). The gigantic beach is still a refuge for all those who want to be alone with the sea and the dunes. Approx. 15 km *(9 mi from Kalkan | entrance fee of 12 lira for the beach; also includes admission to the ancient site of Patara*

SAKLIKENT
(126 B5) (*ØQ F7*)

The gorge of Saklıkent is filled by the ice-cold stream flowing through it that has eaten its way deep into the mountain. If you walk along the water in the narrow ravine you will finally reach a small restaurant built over the river in a deep valley. The gorge itself is always pleasantly cool in summer and therefore makes a welcome change after a fews days on the beach. *Entrance fee 6.25 lira | driving towards Fethiye, there is a signposted road to the right after Pınara, around 35 km (22 mi) from Kalkan*

XANTHOS ⭐
(126 A5) (*ØQ F7*)

Xanthos is the highlight on the path through Lycian history. The former capital of the Lycian Kingdom is still an impressive monument to an ancient culture even though British archaeologists took the most beautiful pieces to London during a 'legal art theft' in the 19th century. The famous Nereid Monument can now be admired in the British Museum in the capital. Today, the ancient city near the village of Kınık is entered through a gate from the Greek period and a Roman triumphal arch that was built in honour of Emperor Vespasian. Tombs, large sarcophaguses, some of which were built back in the 5th century BC, are the main Lycian cultural items that have been preserved. The most impressive is the *Harpy Monument* with a relief showing scenes of the Sirens

Hiking through Saklıkent Canyon

(bird-like creatures) who, in the Lycian religion, took care of the souls of the dead. Lycian graves and remains of the Acropolis can be seen above the Eşen, which was called the Xanthos River in ancient times, while Roman and Byzantine buildings are located to the right of the road. *Daily 8am–7pm | entrance fee 7.50 lira | on the road to Fethiye, turn off at the village of Kınık after around 15 km (9 mi)*

KAŞ

(126 B6) *(㎞ G7–8)* **This town on a large bay far down below the coast road has remained a major destination for back-packers and divers to today.**

Kaş (pop. 7500) is larger than Kalkan but does not have any sandy beaches and has therefore been spared from large hotels.

many holiday complexes on the *Çukurbağ Peninsula* is more suitable if you are looking for a classic beach holiday. Today, Kaş is mainly a realm for divers. There are submarine remains of Lycian settlements in the bays in the vicinity that can be explored. Boats for diving excursions and trips to *Kekova Island* or the Greek island of *Kastellórizo* (Turkish: *Meis*) off the coast leave from the port.

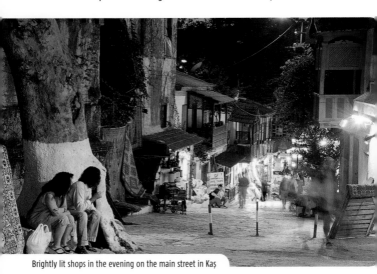

Brightly lit shops in the evening on the main street in Kaş

Many old houses have been preserved in the formerly Greek village that was a rather drowsy place until the 1980s. Lycian sarcophaguses show that Kaş was settled more than 2000 years ago. There is a well-preserved Greek theatre a little way out of town.

Kaş lives from its laid-back cosmopolitan atmosphere, its youthful flair, and the many charming pubs and restaurants. Some of the restaurants have built wooden platforms over the water to make it easy for their guests to dive straight into the sea. Accommodation in one of the

FOOD & DRINK

CHEZ EVY

Good French evening restaurant with novel lamb dishes and delicious desserts. Reservations essential. *Terzi Sok. 2 | tel. 0252 8 36 12 53 | Expensive*

MERCAN RESTAURANT ☀️

The oldest (since 1956) and most distinguished fish restaurant in Kaş is the only place where diners can sit directly next to the water. You can choose your lobster from the aquarium; good starters, fresh fish. *Cumhuriyet Square at the port | tel. 0242 8 36 12 09 | mercankas. net | Expensive*

OBA

Good home-style Turkish cooking in a small *lokanta* near the post office: excellent soups, tasty rice and vegetable dishes, nice garden. *Çukurbağli Cad. 8 | Budget*

SULTAN GARDEN ☼

This garden is located directly on the yacht harbour and has a wonderful view of it. The restaurant is famous for its meat dishes and delicious Turkish appetisers such as *paçanga böreği* (puff pastry with ham). *Yat Limanı | Hükümet Cad. 1 (opposite the coastguard) | tel. 0242 8 36 37 62 | Moderate*

BEACHES

There is no beach in Kaş itself; however, the closest *Küçük Çakıl Plajı* to the east is easy to walk to. You can also take a boat to *Limanağzi*. Day trips to the *Kekova Islands* (see below) and the neighbouring bays are a pleasant alternative.

LEISURE & SPORTS

● Kaş is a diving centre. There are around 15 schools in the town; one of the best is *Barracuda* (see: 'Sports & activities' p. 99). If you prefer to stay above water, you can try out one of the closed, fibreglass boats known as 'sea kayaks'. Paddling, you will be able to explore the ecological system, visit sunken houses and tombs and – with a bit of luck – maybe even meet some seals on the way. The *Dragoman Doga Sporları* travel agency (*Uzunçarşı Cad. 15 | Kaş | tel. 0242 8 36 36 14 | www.dragoman-turkey.com*) offers five-day tours with overnight stays in tents. The proprietors organise won-derful INSIDER TIP mountainbike tours through the thyme fields in the hinterland of Finike. The couple also runs the *Arkandos Mountain Lodge* hotel at an altitude of 243 m (800 ft) and gives mountain bike courses. (*Gökbük Köyü | Finike | tel. 0242 8 62 30 59*). Take the Finike road to Elmalı and turn off after 8 km (5 mi) before Arifler and continue for 1½ km (1 mi)

LOW BUDGET

▶ You can stay in the *Pension Bacchus* in Antalya's Old Town for as little as 32.50 lira a night; simple, but only 50 m to the sea (no beach). 14 rooms | Kılıçaslan Mah., Zeytin Çıkmazi Sok. 6 | tel. 0242 241 69 41 or 0242 243 50 92 | www.bacchus pension.com

▶ You can be sure that the fish you buy at Antalya market are fresh. All stands have a place where you can also eat fish, but make sure they weigh it first! *Kismet Balik Sofrasi | daily noon–9pm | Halk Pazari*

▶ Blue Voyages onboard charter yachts are much cheaper in the off season. *Olympos Yachting* offers three-day cruises in Kaş Bay from around 400 lira/per person (16 May–30 June and 16 Sept–16 Nov). *www. olymposyachting.com*

▶ Weekly markets are held in Kalkan on Thursdays and in Kaş on Fridays. In addition to fruit and vegetables, cheese and herbs from the region and lovely handcrafted articles and fabrics can be purchased at low prices.

KAŞ

ENTERTAINMENT

There are many bars around the port and antique-shop area such as *Janet's Café Bar* and *Café Corner*. *Hi Jazz (Zümrüt Sok. 3)* is the top jazz club in town. *The Red Point Club (Süleyman Topcu Sok. 2)* is a good place to dance to jazz and soul music.

WHERE TO STAY

AQUARIUS

The hotel on the Çukurbağ Peninsula has the best private beach in Kaş; it has been awarded the EU's blue flag for excellent water quality. If you really want to, you can also swim in the pool. *36 rooms | Çukurbağ Yarımadası | tel. 0242 8 36 18 96 | www.aquariushotel.com | Moderate*

INSIDER TIP KAŞ CAMPING ●

The *Hürriyet* newspaper named this the sixth best campsite in Turkey in 2010. *Kaş Camping* offers a comfortable, economical alternative to the hotels in the centre of town. Not far outside town (just 1000 m beyond the theatre) it has good access to the sea. There are also 60 places in tents, caravans and bungalows where you can spend the night on the almost 2 acre property if you don't have your own tent. *Necip Bey Caddesi | tel. 0242 8 36 10 50 | Budget*

OREO

Diving hotel with pool – not only for divers! Only two minutes from the shopping centre. Magnificent garden with olive, pomegranate and lemon trees. *30 rooms | Yaka Mah., Engin Sokak 2 | tel. 0242 8 36 22 20 | www.bt-turkey.com | Budget*

INFORMATION

TURIZM DANIŞMA
Cumhuriyet Meydanı 5 | tel. 0242 8 36 12 38

WHERE TO GO

KASTELLÓRIZO/MEIS
(126 B6) (*Ø G8*)

This picturesque island, with the Greek name of Meyisti that the Turks abbreviated to Meis, is only 3 sea miles from the coast. There has been a partnership between Kaş and Meis since the end of 2006 and the two organise swimming and kayak competitions in late June. The pleasant boat trip alone makes the trip to Dodecanese Island worthwhile, where some pretty pubs await visitors. *Departure from Kaş April–Oct 10am, July–Sept also at 6pm; departure from Meis 3pm and 11.10pm; Nov–March only one crossing daily 10.30am from Kaş and 1.30pm from Meis | tickets 'Meis Express' at the port | tel. 0242 8 36 17 25 | www.meisexpress. com*

Foundations under water: the sunken city off the coast of Kekova

KEKOVA ★ ●
(126 C6) (*Ø H8*)

The island of Kekova, to the east of Kaş, and the strip of coastland opposite it form one of the most fascinating areas on the entire coast. The elongated island lies at the far side of a large bay like a bar closing it in such a way that it appears like an inland lake which, together with its many small islands and rocks, is an impressive sight. There were several settlements on the northern, landward side of Kekova in ancient times; today, some of them are partly under water but still well preserved. You can stand in the water up to your knees and look down at the outline of old houses! All over the bay, Lycian sarcophaguses rise up out of the water and make the atmosphere of this place even more unique. There are two villages on the mainland opposite the island: Üçağız and,

further to the east, *Kaleköy*; the latter is especially inviting for a short stay.

Kaleköy is one of the very few tourist highlights that can still not be reached by car. The only possibility to visit Kaleköy, the historical Simena, is by boat. There are restaurants and – frequently fully booked – guesthouses below the castle built by the Knights of St John of Jerusalem in the Middle Ages; the INSIDER TIP *Kale Pension* (*7 rooms, 1 flat | tel. 0242 8 74 21 11 | www. kalepansiyon.com | Moderate*) is especially charming.

Only a few years ago, there was not much more than a few landing stages from where boats departed for Kaleköy in *Üçağız*. In the meantime, it has developed into a popular destination. People who find Kaş too loud and Kaleköy too remote stay in the lovely guesthouses on the sea here. There are boat tours to the Kekova

Carved in stone: St Nicholas of Myra

times; the present basilica was reconstructed by Tsar Alexander II in the 19th century to show Orthodoxy's profound ties with St Nicholas. A Christian-Islam service is held here at Christmas and attracts many visitors. *Entrance fee around 7.50 lira | 40 km (25 mi) from Kaş towards Finike; turn off to Myra in Kale (a further 1½ km/1 mi*

KEMER

(127 E4–5) (*ⁿ J6*) **Kemer (pop. 17,000) is the centre of an approximately 50 km (31 mi) stretch of coast south-west of Antalya that has developed into a tourist showpiece on the Mediterranean coast** Nothing has remained of what was once a simple fishing village. Kemer is a newly constructed artificial city devoted 100% to tourism (mainly Russians). There are all types of hotels, a new marina, restaurants, cafés and an Aquaworld amusement park in the centre of town. In spite of that, Kemer is not a concrete jungle. The town is generously laid out with a great deal of green and car-free pedestrian precincts – ideal for all who want full service, multilingual waiters, sun sand and the deep blue sea without disappearing behind the fences of the all inclusive holiday complexes.

FOOD & DRINK

Kemer is full of *lokantas* and fast-food restaurants. Menus are always on display and – in spite of the masses of tourists - not overpriced. The restaurants a bit away from the centre are more sophisticated.

APOLLONIK CAFÉ

Here, below the remains of the Apollo Temple, is the place to come and celebrate a heathen ritual at sunset. There is not only

islands every day in summer and they also stop in Kaleköy. *Depart from Kaş on the road to Finike; after 10 km (6 mi) a small road turns off to the left towards Üçağiz.*

MYRA ⭐ (126 C6) (*ⁿ H7*)

Ancient Myra was once an important Lycian city but is now mainly known as the place where St Nicholas was active. The only remnants of the actual Lycian town are the rock tombs, but hardly anywhere else can visitors see as many magnificent examples of these as in Myra. On the steep slope, the so-called house-type tombs – façades carved into the rock with the actual graves hidden behind them – are clustered one next to the other. The INSIDER TIP ▶ *St Nicholas Basilica* is located below Myra in *Kale* (known earlier as Demre). It was originally built in the Byzantine period and destroyed several

beer and wine, but also coffee and tea. *Nar Sok. 69 | tel. 0242 7 53 10 70 | Moderate*

INSIDER **TIP** **ÇINAR**

The oldest – and best – garden restaurant a little outside Kemer serves excellent meat dishes as well as delicious fish. The baked trout straight out of the oven are fabulous! *Ulupınar (on the road from Kemer to Kumluca, approx. 20 km/12½ mi) | tel. 0242 8 25 00 29 | Moderate*

YÖRÜK PARK

Yörük Park on the promontory in the marina serves food in an unusual setting. You can enjoy a typical meal in an open-air museum where the life of the nomads – who used to live between the coast and meadows of the Taurus Mountains – is depicted. It is also worth visiting even if you are not hungry. *At the marina | tel. 0242 8 14 17 77 | www.yorukparki.com.tr | Moderate*

SHOPPING

The main road down to the marina is quite simply just a row of shops. *Element Deri (Liman Cad. 17A)* and *Lederland* *(Sariören Mah., Turizm Cad.)* have a good selection of leather goods.

BEACHES

Kemer has a beach on its doorstep. This continues towards Antalya with *Göynük* and *Beldibi,* and *Çamyuva* and *Tekirova* to the south. Excursion boats depart for the beaches from the marina in Kemer in the morning.

ENTERTAINMENT

People get together at the street bazaar, the port and in Moonlight Park *(Ayışığı Parkı)* after 10pm and then go to a bar or dancing at one of the discotheques such as *Inferno*; locations close at around 5 in the morning.

KAPTAN TERAS BAR ☘

Things are a little more peaceful here on the terrace with the lovely view of the port. *At the end of Deniz Caddesi.*

MOON BAR

Popular meeting place for culture lovers. Artists from the State Opera in Ankara

ST NICHOLAS & SANTA CLAUS

St Nicholas is an Orthodox Byzantine saint. At the heyday of the Byzantine era, around 1000 AD, Nicholas was highly revered in what was then Constantinople. The legend of Santa Claus who puts sweets and other goodies into children's stockings is actually based on a historical figure. Nicholas lived around 300–350 AD and was bishop of Myra for a time. Although the Byzantine church saw him as the patron saint of seafarers, his fame

is based on the legend of the three daughters of a poor man who, it is said, had no dowry for his children. Nicholas threw a purse full of gold into the poor man's house three years in a row at around Christmas time. Some say that the gold came down the chimney. In many countries, St Nicholas' day is on 6 December – the day the bishop of Myra died – and in others, Santa Claus distributes his presents on Christmas Eve.

perform here every evening in the high season. *Ayışığı Parkı | tel. 0242 8 14 49*

SIR WILLIAMS
One of the good English pubs. *Ayışığı Parkı | tel. 0242 8 14 48 41*

WHERE TO STAY

Most of the hotels are booked as part of a package. Information on the main hotels in Kemer can be found under *www.hotel guide.com.tr*

NATURLAND ECOPARK HOTELS
A quartet in Çamyuva Bay. The complexes comprise *Aquarium Park (133 rooms), Country Park (80 rooms), Forest Park (170 rooms)* and *Naturvillas (83 rooms)*. The concept is to be close to nature, offer fresh fruit and vegetables and keep small animals. *Çamyuva | tel. 0242 8 24 62 14 | www. naturland.com.tr | Expensive*

RIXOS SUNGATE PORT ROYAL
This is one of the largest holiday complexes in Turkey and has recently been renovated. Stylish, cheerful, laid-back atmosphere. INSIDER TIP Beautiful poolside rooms. *1094 rooms | Çifteçeşmeler Mevkii | Beldibi | tel. 0242 8 24 00 00 | www.rixos.com | Moderate*

INFORMATION

TURIZM DANIŞMA
Yat Limani 159 | tel. 0242 8 14 11 12 | www. antalya-kemer.bel.tr

WHERE TO GO

KUZDERE (127 E4) (*ØJ J6*)
The village of Kuzdere, 10 km (6 mi) northwest of Kemer, is the starting point for excursions to the Taurus Mountains. This is where you depart for the *Beydağları*

National Park, this is where the unmade road to *Tahtalı Dağ*, the former Mount Olympos, begins, as does a beautiful 25 km-long (15½ mi) hiking or mountain-bike trail to INSIDER TIP *Kuzdere Yaylası*, a mountain pasture where semi-nomadic shepherds still graze their sheep. Hiking boots are a must! *www.kemer-tr.info/ kuzdere.htm | shared taxis from Kemer bus station*

OLYMPOS (127 E5) (*ØJ J7*)
The name Olympos is connected with more than just one of the many ancient sites on the Mediterranean coast. Olympos is the name of the town in Antiquity as well as the one the Greeks in Asia Minor gave to this mountain (today: *Tahtalı Dağ; see below*) and a fantastic conservation area and holiday region. There are a few villages with small guesthouses in the vicinity of Olympos. If you take the road from Kemer to Finike, there is a signpost to Çıralı on the left. After a few miles along a winding road you reach Çıralı on the beach of Olympos. This is still an almost untouched natural beauty; however, there is no sand but only pebbles. You can stay in the luxurious *Olympos Lodge (12 rooms | tel. 0242 8 25 71 71 | www.olymposlodge.com.tr | Expensive)* or *Şaban Pension* where you sleep in tree houses *(tel. 0242 8 92 12 65 | www.sabanpension.com | Budget)* in Çıralı. The campsite is a fine alternative.
The *Eternal Flames* (Turkish: *yanartaş*), the place where the mythical figure – the chimera – lives, are located to the north of Çıralı. You can either take a guided tour from Çıralı or climb the mountain following the signs on your own. A INSIDER TIP night hike, when the flames fed by the gas coming out of the slope of the mountain can be seen from afar, is a fascinating alternative. *Entrance fee 12.50 lira | 7 km (4½mi) walk or taxi ride from the main road (signposted); Yanartaş lies at an a*

titude of almost 180 m (590 ft) at the northern end of Çirali Beach, 3 km (1¾mi) inland; the first half of the road is open to traffic – you have to walk the rest | www.kemer-info.tr

PHASELIS ⭐ (127 E5) (*Ø J7*)

The ancient city with three harbours in the middle of a forest was already used by the Phoenicians as a trading centre. However, the first official records of Phaselis as a city only date from around 700 BC when people from Rhodes settled here. A visit to Phaselis, only 12 km (7½ mi) to the south of Kemer, provides an opportunity to see interesting ancient sites and to swim in this impressive setting. You can now swim in the former harbours in which the remains of the old docks can still be seen beneath the water. *Entrance fee 15 lira | minibuses from Kemer bus station | www.lycianturkey.com*

The INSIDER TIP *Sundance Nature Village* with bungalows, treehouses and a wonderful deserted stretch of beach is located at the southwest. There is electricity and air conditioning but no telephone or television. The eggs come from the village, the vegetables grown in the grounds without the use of pesticides and the jam is homemade *(tel. 0242 8 21 41 65 | www.sundancecamp.com).*

TAHTALI DAĞ (127 E5) (*Ø J7*)

Tahtalı ('The Wooden') is the name given to the highest peak (2366 m/7762 ft) of this section of the Taurus Mountains where they come closest to the sea. A lift was opened in 2007 and it is now possible to cover the almost 4.5 km (3 mi) to the peak in a mere 15 minutes. The cabins take up to 80 passengers. At the top, sunbeds and a café restaurant await you in the sunshine. A path leads down from the top to the village of *Beycik* (at 850 m/ 2800 ft) in the southwest. You will come across many rare species of flower along this hiking path including the Anatolian orchid *(Orchis anatolica).* Turn right from the road to Kaş after Çamyuva; the lift is signposted and reached along a 7 km (4½ mi) tarmac road through the wood | minibuses from Kemer (15 km/9½ mi) April–Oct 8am–7pm, every 30 minutes, last departure from the top 7pm (in winter, 6pm) | Tahtalı Teleferiki | Cumhuriyet Meydani 1/6 | Kemer-Antalya | tel. 0242 8 14 30 47 | www.tahtali.com/english

The magnificent view from the ancient theatre in Phaselis

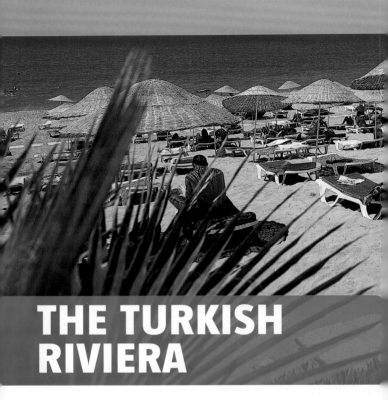

THE TURKISH RIVIERA

When people talk about the Turkish Riviera, they usually mean the endless sandy beaches between Antalya and Alanya. Most of the 'all inclusive' holiday complexes where tourists from the north come to enjoy the sun, beach and sea are located along this 150 km (93 mi) stretch of the coast.

But ancient Pamphylia has much more to offer: one of the largest Roman theatres in the world in Aspenndos, the Temple of Apollo in Side, a pirates' castle in Alanya, rivers and canyons inland, and the Taurus Mountains that can be seen from everywhere that provide protection from the cold north winds, guaranteeing a mild climate throughout the year. That's why oranges, lemons and vegetables have been cultivated to the east of Antalya for centuries. Today, large greenhouses make it possible to harvest tomatoes, aubergines and lettuces throughout the year. When the cotton bursts open in late summer it looks as if it has snowed – even though the temperature is around 30° C (86° F).

ALANYA

MAP INSIDE BACK COVER
(131 D4) (*ⴒ N6–7*) Alanya (pop. 95,000), the most easterly point on the

Mediterranean hospitality, sea, sand and sunshine galore – and one of the best-preserved theatres of Antiquity

Turkish Riviera, has become the German stronghold on the Mediterranean coast. The attractive location of the well cared-for city with its lovely beaches and the impressive citadel on a hill in the centre of town is well on the way to becoming a small version of Mallorca.

Nowhere else have so many Germans settled as here. In the meantime, there are more than 20,000 spread throughout

CITY **WHERE TO START?**
At the mosque: orientate yourself on the upper and lower towns, the castle hill and modern city. The road to the upper town starts at Kulularönu Camii. From the foot of the hill, the sandy beaches, bazaar and port are just a few minutes away.

the region. This is mainly due to the climate as winter hardly exists in Alanya; the temperature almost never falls below 10° C (50° F), the sea is warm all year round and oranges and bananas can be picked here when snow falls in northern Europe. Ex-pats not only have a good relationship with each other but also to the communal authorities. A cancer clinic and other health services are the result of the German migration to the Turkish Riviera — and German has now almost become the second official language in Alanya.

A large pedestrian precinct has developed next to the small Old Town district. The palm-lined promenade leads past tea gardens and the traffic is even a little less chaotic than in other places in Turkey. You reach the old port at the end of the promenade where the Red Tower (*Kızıl Kule*)

acts as a reminder that Alanya was once an important military base.

Alanya lies at the moth of two important rivers: Dim and Kargı. In ancient times, cedar from the Taurus Mountains was floated down to the coast down these rivers before being transported to the Egyptian shipyards in Alexandria.

SIGHTSEEING

ALANYA KALESI ★ ● ⛌

The fortress, 300 m (985 ft) above the sea, was frequently extended throughout history on account of its commanding position. Most of the walls and ramparts that can still be seen are the remains of the complex with 150 towers built by the Seljuks in the 13th century. There are also sections of a Byzantine basilica and remnants of a large cistern to be seen inside

Damlataş Mağarasi: in the cave near Alanya

İç Kale. The most impressive are the ramparts towards the sea with a large viewing platform where executions were once carried out and which now offers a magnificent view of the Mediterranean. *Daily 8am–5pm | entrance fee 11.25 lira*

ARKEOLOJI MÜZESI

The small municipal museum displays archaeological finds as well as Seljuk and Ottoman arts and crafts. In addition, there are collections of beautiful old kilims, coins and calligraphy. The bronze statue of Hercules from the 2nd century AD is especially noteworthy. *Atatürk Park, corner Güzelyalı Caddesi | daily 8am–5pm | entrance fee 5 lira*

CAVES

There are several caves at the foot of the fortress hill but only the largest of them, *Damlataş Mağarası*, at the end of Atatürk Park can be reached from the land. The *Pirates Cave*, *Lovers Cave* and ★ *Phosphorescent Cave*, with its amazing light reflections, are only accessible by boat from the port. *(Cave tour approx. 25 lira).*

KIZIL KULE

The Red Tower is the symbol of the city and was erected by the Seljuk Sultan Alaeddin Kekkubat in 1224. The 35 m (115 ft) high, octagonal brick tower forms the corner of the harbour fortifications. Today, there is a small folklore museum on the ground floor. *Daily 8am–5pm | entrance fee 6.25 lira*

TERSANE

If you set out on a boat trip to the caves, you should be sure to also visit the old Seljuk shipyards. The sultans had their naval fleet built in five huge caverns cut deep into the hill. The wood came from the forests in the Taurus. The docks provided a haven for the fleet, making Alanya

one of the safest harbours in the eastern Mediterranean. *Tours from the port, approx. 3 hours | 25–40 lira*

FOOD & DRINK

HANCI PATISSERIE
Good tea, coffee and cakes at a reasonable price – this chain of pastry shops has developed into an institution in Alanya. Also a good place for breakfast. Main shop: *Hasan Akcalioğlu Cad. 9 | tel. 0242 5 13 70 70 | Budget*

ÖZ GRAND RESTAURANT
The best kebab house in Alanya also serves fish and French food. *Çimen Oteli Sokak | tel. 0242 5 11 93 18 | Moderate*

RED TOWER BREWERY
Restaurant with its own brewery and good plain Turkish cooking. Excellent salads as

---

MARCO POLO HIGHLIGHTS

★ **Alanya Kalesi**
The former pirates' citadel on the fortress cliff in Alanya dominates the coastline → p. 72

★ **Phosphorescent Cave**
The caves in Alanya's fortress hill were used for secret trysts and as shipyards → p. 73

★ **Temple of Apollo**
The temple at the tip of the promontory in Side is a must at sunset → p. 77

★ **Aspendos**
Concerts and opera performances are still held in the largest Roman theatre preserved in the eastern Mediterranean area → p. 78

well as kebabs. The restaurant is at the port and has room for around 100 guests. *İskele Caddesi 80 | tel. 0242 5 13 66 64 | www.redtowerbrewery.com | Moderate*

BEACHES

Alanya's beaches stretch almost 3 km (1¾ mi) to the west and nearly 8 km (3 mi) eastwards. *Cleopatra Beach* west of Fortress Hill has the cleanest water. If you travel a couple of miles towards Antalya, you will reach the famous *İncekum Beach* between Konaklı and Avşalar with a campsite and *İncekum Recreation Park* next to the sea.

LOW BUDGET

▶ You can try Alanya's famous cooking quite cheaply in Esma Abla's restaurant. *Closed Sun | Saray Mahallesi, Galatasaray Cad. 56/A–B Uysal. Apt. | Alanya | tel. 0242 5 19 08 40*

▶ Alanya is a good place to spend the winter – for example in the 3-star Hotel Ikiz at Cleopatra Beach: from 20 lira per person, 32 lira with half-board. *32 rooms | Kızlarpınarı Mahallesi, Atatürk Cad. Belen Sok. 3 | tel. 0242 5 13 31 55 | www.ikizotel.com*

▶ An excursion to the large waterfall at Manavgat is not expensive and a lot of fun. The entrance fee is only 2.50 lira. If you want, you can pay 5 lira and have a photograph taken of you sitting on a camel.

▶ Between 9pm–11pm drinks are much cheaper every evening in the *Lighthouse disco* at Side harbour.

LEISURE & SPORTS

An international volleyball tournament is held at the end of May every year on Cleopatra Beach where a grandstand for 5000 spectators is erected. This kind of activity continues with handball at the end of June and a beach football championship in the second half of July. However, the highlight is the triathlon with rafting (3 km/1¾ mi), mountain biking (13 km/8 mi) and running (5 km/3 mi) in October. *www.alanyacup.com*

ENTERTAINMENT

As in all the other resort towns on the coast there is a row of pubs and discos at the port and along the promenade *(İskele Caddesi).* The most popular are *Bellman, James Dean* and *Zapfhahn*. There are some other pubs in the side streets towards the centre including *Doors* and *Murphy's* fo the not-so-young. It is also possible to eat in *Queen's Garden (Demirciler Sokak).* In addition, there are some bars with Turkish live music in the centre of Alanya such as *Ada (Atatürk Cad.)* and *Boomerang (İzzet Azakoğlu Cad.).*

WHERE TO STAY

ANFORA RESIDENCE

Apartment hotel with two and three roomed holiday flats, with views of the large swimming pool or the sea, sleeping up to a maximum of 7. Cleopatra Beach is 50 m away and the town centre just 2 km (1¼ mi). Breakfast or half-board available if required. *110 flats | Kemali Soydan Cad. | tel. 0242 5 14 10 66 | www.anfora hotel.com | Budget–Moderate*

DINLER

Massive building with private beach on Kargıcak Bay to the south. Open all-year

The lighting is perfect: James Dean Bar in Alanya

round with indoor and outdoor pools. *172 rooms | Kargıcak Beldesi | tel. 0242 5 26 20 94 | www.dinler.com | Moderate– Expensive*

SEA PORT HOTEL
Maritime boutique hotel above the port: ask for a room with a sea view! *65 rooms | İskele Cad. 82 | tel. 0242 5 13 64 87 | www.hotelseaport.com | Moderate*

YOGA ASHRAM ●
The meditation centre looks down on the magnificent valley of the River Dim. Yogi Adnan Çabuk and his wife Lourdes Doplito offer relaxation exercises and organic food. Electronic equipment is forbidden. The river is there for yoga, swimming and purifying the soul. *20 beds | 30 km (18 mi) from Alanya | only open July–Sept | bookings: tel. 0212 2 30 15 47 or 0533 7 77 86 40 | www.siddashramyogacenter.com | Moderate*

INFORMATION

TURIZM DANIŞMA
Damlataş Caddesi 1 | tel. 0242 5 13 12 40 | www.info-alanya.com, www.alanya.bel.tr

WHERE TO GO

ALARA HAN (130 C4) (*M6*)
The best preserved *caravanserai* from the Seljuk period on the Silk Road was built on the River Alara on the behest of Sultan Alaeddin Keykubat in 1231. This used to be part of the route from Alanya to the capital city of Konya. The building consists of massive outer walls and a large inner courtyard from where the stables on the ground floor and the rooms for the guides and the caravan guards could be reached via a gallery. INSIDERTIP Alara Fortress lies like a swallow's nest stuck to the rock face high above the *caravanserai*. The fortress can be reached by a narrow path

and you will be rewarded with a ☀ magnificent view from the top. The River Alara is also perfect for a refreshing swim before eating a freshly-caught trout *(alabalık)* in one of the restaurants. *Towards Antalya, turn off to the right after 35 km (22 mi) | entrance free*

INSIDER TIP ▶ DIM ÇAYI
(131 D4) *(𝄞 N–O6)*

The trip to this small river around 10 km (6 mi) to the east of Alanya makes a lovely change from the daily sunbathing session on the beach. You can take a short stroll in the shade of the trees and eat in one of the local restaurants. The river has been dammed and the area has now become a popular place for recreation. It is usually around 10 degrees cooler here than in Alanya; you can hire canoes or swim in the ice-cold water. *Can be reached by dolmuş taxi from Alanya.*

SIDE

MAP INSIDE BACK COVER
(130 B3–4) *(𝄞 L–M6)* **Modernday Side (pop. 6500) is right next to the Roman theatre and is practically in the middle of the ancient town.**

Just like 3000 years ago, you first pass through a town wall that protects the peninsula on the landward side and then drive along the road of columns past the Agora to a car park next to the theatre. The restored *Temple of Apollo* facing the sea at the tip of the peninsula, which is closed to traffic, gives an idea of the city's former size. From here, take a walk through the narrow streets, past hundreds of shops, restaurants, bars and guesthouses to the ancient harbour of Side.

Side was colonised by the Greeks in the 7th century BC. It became an important harbour at that time and was fought over by Greeks, Persians, Romans and Cilician pirates. The city had many rulers in its eventful history but that never stopped the people who lived here going about their business.

In the meantime, Side has experienced an invasion of another kind. An increasing number of visitors come every year and, in summer, the shopping area is more like a fairground where the Greek temples, Roman baths and Byzantine basilicas disappear into the background. The city has become a place where package holidaymakers who stay in large hotel complexes in the Side area go out and have fun at night. The all-inclusive hotels near town have also become popular with northern

Chillout: restaurant in Dim Çayi

Symbol of the city: Temple of Apollo in Side

European pensioners as a place to spend the winter.

SIGHTSEEING

The ancient city of Side is one of the most attractive excavated areas in Turkey. Once you have parked your car next to the well preserved *Roman theatre* that used to accommodate 15,000 people you can either take the 'tractor train' through the excavation site or stroll along the road lined with columns *(entrance fee 12.50 lira)*. The former market, the *Agora*, is well preserved; there is also a *Vespasian Monument* from the Roman era and an *Archaeological Museum* is now located in the erstwhile Byzantine baths *(Tue–Sun 8am–noon and 1pm–5pm entrance fee 7.50 lira)*. However, Side's major ancient highlight is the – at least, partially – reconstructed ★ ● *Temple of Apollo* (2nd century AD) directly on the beach that offers a magnificent panoramic scene in front of the setting sun. During the high season, INSIDER TIP concerts are held in the theatre and near the temple.

FOOD & DRINK

APOLLONIK CAFÉ
The café for your aperitif in the evening – and the best place to enjoy the sunset with a view of the Temple of Apollo. *Liman Cad. | tel. 0242 7 53 10 70 | Moderate*

DEUTSCHES STEAK HOUSE
Excellent steaks on the terrace with a view of Side and the west beach. *Yasemin Sokak | tel. 0242 7 53 36 14 | Moderate*

PAŞAKÖY

The restaurant has a quiet garden in the midst of all the hustle and bustle; good barbeque, light cooking – and cheap. *Liman Cad. | tel. 0242 753 36 22 | Budget*

SOUNDWAVES

People who want to eat well in Side almost always end up in this restaurant with Turkish and international food. Vegetables served in a clay pot are especially tasty. *Küçük Plaj (on the east promenade) | tel. 0242 753 10 59 | Moderate*

BEACHES

The Side peninsula has large sandy beaches on both sides. Those who choose the east beach swim right in front of the ruins of the ancient city. *Sorgun*, with an endless landscape of dunes with a pine forest in the background, is 3 km (2 mi) to the east. *Minibuses every 30 minutes from the bus station (Otogar)*

ENTERTAINMENT

The area around the bazaar with one bar after the next in the centre of Side turns into something of a funfair every evening. The *Lighthouse* open-air disco at the port is a good place to go dancing. Those looking for something a little more tranquil will enjoy the many open-air cafés and pubs at the tip of the peninsula near the Temple of Apollo.

WHERE TO STAY

INSIDER TIP ▶ BEACH HOUSE HOTEL

The Turkish-Australian couple Ali and Penny Yesilipek and their son Alan run this hotel, built on the site of an old Byzantine villa on the outskirts of Side. There is a small, but lovely, stretch of beach with umbrellas and sunbeds. The rooms facing the sea have charming balconies and the *Soundwaves* restaurant is in the same building. *20 rooms | Barbaros Caddesi | tel. 0242 753 16 07 | www.beachhouse-hotel.com | Budget–Moderate*

HOTEL VILLA ÖNEMLI

Cheerful, new hotel in the style of a wooden bungalow directly on the sea. It has a large garden and is lovingly run by the Önemlis. *14 rooms, 1 flat | Küçük Plaj Üstü | Köyiçi Mevkii, Lale Sok. | tel. 0242 753 28 60 | www.hotelvillaonemli.com | Moderate*

YÜKSER PANSIYON

Old house in the centre of Side with an easy-going atmosphere and lovely garden, only 50 m from the beach. *8 rooms | Sümbül Sok. 8 | tel. 0242 753 20 10 | www.yukser-pansiyon.com | Budget*

INFORMATION

TURIZM DANIŞMA

Side Yolu Üzeri | Manavgat | tel. 0242 753 12 65

WHERE TO GO

ASPENDOS ★ ● (124 A3) (ᗏ L5)

Aspendos is the largest and best-preserved Roman theatre in the eastern Mediterranean. There is still room for an audience of around 20,000 people when the concert season starts in June. In Roman times, Aspendos was a major trading centre and a large aqueduct has been preserved in addition to the theatre. The fact that the gigantic theatre is in such good condition after 1800 years is due to the fact that the Seljuks used it as a *caravanserai* and took good care of it. A visit to a concert in this theatre is a truly unique experience. *(www.aspendosfestival.gov.tr). Entrance fee 18.75 lira | on the main*

The wide curtain of the Manavgat Falls

road towards Antalya as far as Belkis, sign-posted at the junction to the right, 20 km (12½ mi)

INSIDER TIP ▶ **BELEK** (130 A3) *(᠓ L6)*

This elegant holiday centre with one luxury hotel after the next has been created in the middle of a pine forest half way between Side and Antalya. Belek's golf resorts are among the best in the world and dozens of golf courses have been established in the surrounding area. The beach resort of Belek is actually a part of the small village of Kadriye that is developing into a tourist centre and already has quite a few shops and restaurants. *www.betuyab.org | on the main road to Antalya, turn left towards Kadriye/Belek after Serik, 35 km (22 mi)*

MANAVGAT (130 B3–4) *(᠓ M6)*

Manavgat is the modern municipality that Side, 10 km (6¼mi) away, is actually a part of. Famous for its waterfalls, the town lives less from tourism than from

agriculture. The produce of the surrounding area is sold at the large market on Mondays.

Coming from Side, the route to the main waterfall on the Manavgat River branches off at the entrance to the town. You reach the waterfall after 3 km (1¾mi) but the restaurants and car parks on the way will make you aware of this beforehand. The falls are not especially high but the river is so wide here that it is still a very impressive spectacle. An outing can be made even more perfect by sampling a freshly-caught trout in one of the restaurants. If you still have time and a car, you can drive further along the road by the river and after about 15 km (9 mi) you will reach the first of two reservoirs, *Oymapınar Barajı*, where you can take a break in the pleasant garden restaurant *Şahin Cafeteria (Oymapınar Beldesi | tel. 0242 7 72 20 10 | Budget)*. *Minibuses to the waterfall depart from the bus station (Otogar); there are also excursion boats from the port (45 lira)*

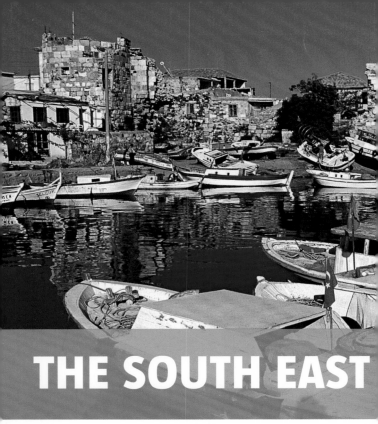

THE SOUTH EAST

Beach holidays end to the east of Alanya; this is where a region of fascinating discoveries begins. There are beaches between Anamur and Antakya but the coast is still little developed for tourism and has remained a terra incognita for package holiday-makers – to the delight of individualists.

Cilicia, as the coast between Alanya and Mersin was called in ancient times, has a lot to offer. Byzantines and Seljuks, Armenians and Crusaders, Arabs and Ottomans have all left their traces here. The stretch of coast to the east of Adana that juts into Syria like a finger was the scene of three events of worldwide his-

torical importance. The great battle between the Hittites and pharaonic Egyptians took place here in 1285 BC; in 333 BC, Alexander the Great celebrated his decisive victory over the Persians (at the Battle of Issus) and, a good 300 years later, a handful of people gathered in a cave near Antakya – known as Antioch at that time – to establish a new religion. They called themselves Christians and their spiritual leader was none less than St Peter the Apostle.

The landscape of the coast is divided into three sections. From Alanya to Silifke, the lovely coast road passes through an area which has barely been settled where ba-

Photo: Fishing port in Adana

In the footsteps of the first Christians: Turkey's eastern Mediterranean coast boasts ancient churches and plenty of sun

nanas grow on terraced slopes. From time to time, you will come across delightful beaches. The main industrial region of southern Turkey starts beyond Silifke. Mersin and İskenderun are commercial and military harbours and Adana, a city with a population of well over one million, is the centre of the country's cotton and textile industry. It is only to the south of İskenderun, a city founded by Alexander the Great after a victory and named Alexandreia at the time, that visitors once again discover a tranquil stretch of coast with beautiful scenery and a fascinating cultural history and the provincial capital of Antakya further inland. The province of Antakya (or Hatay) still has a strong Arab influence and the city of the same name is the most oriental town on the entire south coast.

Most of the Kurds have only migrated to Adana over the past thirty years, attracted by the flourishing commercial metropolis and displaced from their former homes by the battles between the Turkish Army and the Kurdish separatists of the illegal PKK (Kurdistan Workers' Party). The city has a subtropical climate and temperatures can reach 45° C (113° F) at the height of summer; the luxuriant vegetation in the parks is just one sign of this. There is not much evidence of Adana's long history – the first archaeological finds date from the Hittite period around 1600 BC. The oldest preserved construction is a bridge over the Seyhan that Emperor Hadrian had built in 117 AD. The Roman stone bridge makes a strong contrast to the city's newest sight, the enormous Sabancı Mosque in the centre. Adana's most prominent family has erected a monument to itself with this Ottoman-style mosque. The Sabancı dynasty's wealth comes from cotton from the Çukurova and today it controls the second largest industrial holding in Turkey. The city is also famous internationally for the nearby US military airport in Incirlik, one of the largest air force bases outside of the USA. In addition, the Yumurtalık oil terminal, where oil pipelines from Iraq and the Baku-Ceyhan pipeline meet and their oil is pumped into tankers, is located

Mighty dome: Sabanci Mosque

ADANA

(134 C3) *(Ω X5)* **Adana (pop. 2 million) is the fourth largest city in Turkey and, along with Antalya, the fastest growing metropolis in the country. Adana is the trading centre for the agricultural production of the Çukzrova Plain and centre of the textile industry that processes the cotton grown on the lowlying plains nearby.**

You will discover Adana as an unpretentious, south-Anatolian city. The population is made up of Turks, Arabs and Kurds.

> **WHERE TO START?**
> **Kemeraltı Mosque:** The main meeting place in the metropolis of Adana is the Kemeraltı Camii on the central Küçük Saat Meydanı square. The Old Town and bazaar lie along the street to Taş Köprü (bridge). The Archaeological Museum and bus station can also be easily reached from here.

to the south of Adana. The oil terminal is in the delta of the Ceyhan that, along with the Seyhan that flows into the sea a little further to the west, forms the Çukurova alluvial plain. This plain is where the Turkish cotton industry has its roots and has developed into one of the most profitable areas for cultivating cotton and grain in the world.

SIGHTSEEING

ADANA ARKEOLOJI MÜZESI ●
The Archaeological Museum was founded in 1924 as one of the very first in the Turkish Republic. It concentrates on the finds from the Hittite and Roman periods that were unearthed in so-called *höyüks*, archaeological mounds on the plain. The statues, stone tablets and mosaics are exhibited in a somewhat old-fashioned way but are definitely worth seeing. *Tue–Sun 8.30am–5pm | entrance fee 6 lira*

SABANCI MERKEZ CAMII
Six minarets 99 metres (325 ft) high, a gigantic dome with a diameter of 32 m (105 ft) and space for 12,000 worshippers – these are the impressive figures of the traditional Sabancı Mosque that was built in 1998. *On the west bank of the Seyhan*

FOOD & DRINK

YÜZEVLER KEBAP SALONU
Adana is the home of the spicy INSIDER TIP Adana Kebap that has become a speciality throughout Turkey. But, of course, it tastes best here. First of all, shepherd's salad, parsley, grated carrots, lettuce, spices, onions and warm flat bread are served. You can also order it with cacik and mint. Eating a kebap can easily turn into a quite a ritual. *Ziyapaşa Bulvarı 25/A | tel. 0322 4 54 75 31 | www.yuzevler.com.tr | Moderate*

BEACHES

The seaside resort *Karataş*, to which the people of Adana flock on scorching summer days, is south of the city. *Yumurtalik*, on the coast to the east, is more attractive and an ideal place to go for a swim as the oil terminals are some way away. Yumurtalik still has the charm of an old fishing village and is surrounded by ruins from Armenian times.

WHERE TO STAY

AKKOÇ BUTIK OTEL
Spotlessly clean, modern city hotel in the centre. Room service, satellite TV, breakfast buffet, good restaurant. *30 rooms | Cemalpaşa Mah., 63005 Sok. 22 | tel. 0322 4 59 10 00 | www.akkocotel.com.tr | Moderate*

MARCO POLO HIGHLIGHTS

★ **Mamure Kalesi**
The medieval fortress is one of the most impressive buildings in Turkey → p. 85

★ **Antakya Müzesi**
The museum in Antakya has one of the largest collections of Roman mosaics in the world → p. 87

★ **Church of St Peter the Apostle**
Peter the Apostle founded the first Christian community in the cave church in Antakya → p. 88

★ **Kiz Kalesi**
The 'Maiden's Castle' in the sea to the south of Silifke can only be reached by boat today → p. 91

INFORMATION

TOURISM OFFICE

Yerni Valilik Binasi (in the Governor's Office) Block C, 3rd & 4th floor | tel. 0322 4 58 84 28 | adana@kulturturizm.gov.tr

WHERE TO GO

ANAVARZA ☀ **(135 D2)** *(ᗰ Y4)*

This former Armenian fortress complex is located some 60 km (37 mi) northeast of Adana. The ruins on the 200 m (655 ft) high hill can be seen from far away on the fertile plain and open up a spectacular panoramic view of the entire surrounding countryside. There are still relics of the city that was founded in the 1st century AD in the area around the fortress hill. High-quality honey is produced here organically and sold under the name of 'Anavarza'.

ANAMUR

(131 F6) *(ᗰ P8)* **The provincial centre of Anamur (pop. 50,000 including the neighbouring villages) is still largely untouched by tourism. It is located around 6 km (4 mi) inland from the coast.**

Anamur is especially famous for its bananas, peanuts, citrus fruit and strawberries. There are many inland villages where Turkmen nomads still live and make a modest living from carpet weaving and wood carving. The city dwellers also escape to their summer houses surrounded by mountain pastures when the temperatures rise to more than 40° C (104° F) in the hot season.

Anamur is the right place to visit if you want to find out about everyday life in a small town in the provinces unspoiled by tourism. Anamur İskele, a suburb on the

BOOKS & FILMS

▶ **Memed, My Hawk** – Yaşar Kemal, the most famous contemporary writer in Turkey, tells the story of a young rebel in the Adana region and his struggle against the omnipotence of the big landowners.

▶ **Birds without Wings** – this love story, written by Louis de Bernières, also tells of the emergence of modern Turkey seen through the eyes of the residents of a small village in southwestern Turkey as they witness the collapse of the Ottoman Empire.

▶ **The Museum of Innocence** – by Orhan Pamuk, the Nobel-laureate Turkish novelist, was published in 2008. A challenging read about an obsessive

love, this novel paints a vivid picture of the emerging modernity of Istanbul in the 1970s.

▶ **From Russia with Love** – the 1963 the film based on the Ian Fleming novel is perhaps the most famous film set in Turkey. Directed by Terrence Young and starring Sean Connery, most of the film was shot on Turkish soil.

▶ **The Crossing (2010)** – Selim Demirdelen's film about a father and daughter, was screened at a number of international film festivals across the globe and won several awards at the 17th Adana 'Golden Boll' International Film Festival.

Mamure Kaleşi, Anamur's crusader castle was built in the 12th century

seashore about 4 km (2½mi) away, is a different story – at least, during the holiday season. It has developed into a hotspot for local tourists with hotels and restaurants on the lovely sandy beach *(minibuses from the bust station from 7am).* Anamur's real highlights are outside the town: the large crusaders' fortress *Mamure Kalesi* on a peninsula to the east of Anamur and the *Anemourion* ruins in the southwest. In addition, fascinating caves with stalactites wait to be explored.

SIGHTSEEING

ANAMUR MÜZESI

The small museum in the İskele district mainly displays exhibits from nearby fortress, Anemourion. *Tue–Sun 8.30am–12.30pm, 1.30pm–5.30pm | entrance fee 3.75 lira | Yalıevler Mah., Fahri Görgülü Cad. 8 | www.kultur.gov.tr*

ANEMOURION

This fortress, built by Armenian princes on the cliffs above the beach on the southernmost tip of the Turkish mainland, is an impressive sight. The picturesque 'Stormy Place', as the Greeks called it, looks back over a long history that began with Greek colonists and ended with the Ottomans. The citadel was built in the 12th century; the remains of the settlement are from the Roman and Byzantine periods. It is said that is possible to see as far as Cyprus about 70 km (44 mi) to the south if the weather is fine. *Daily except Mon | entrance fee 6 lira | signposted turnoff to Anemourion after 5 km (3 mi) along the Antalya road*

MAMURE KALESI ★

This castle, built on a rocky promontory and washed by the sea on three sides, is the best-preserved and most beautiful crusaders' fortress on the Turkish south coast. The citadel, built by German master craftsmen in the 12th century, was used for military purposes until modern times and renovated once again by the Ottomans in the 19th century. Its gigantic walls are well-preserved. The walkways are still passable and you will be rewarded with a fine view of the entire complex if you climb up to the tower on the seaward side. *Tue–Sun 9am–5pm | entrance fee 5 lira | 6 km (3¾mi) east of Anamur | dolmuş from the bus station*

FOOD & DRINK

ANEMONIA RESTAURANT
The restaurant in the hotel of the same name on the beach serves good meat and fish dishes. *İskele Mahallesi, İnönü Cad. | tel. 0324 8 14 40 00 | Moderate*

KAP ANAMUR
Charming restaurant on the terrace of the Kap Anamur Hotel. This is a good place to enjoy fresh fish in a pleasant atmosphere. *İskele Mahallesi, İnönü Cad. | tel. 0324 8 14 23 47 | Moderate*

WHERE TO STAY

ESER PANSIYON
Pleasant hotel with large balconies and low prices. You can make prepare your coffee in the shared kitchen; breakfast and dinner are eaten in the shade of the vines on the terrace with a view of the sea. *11 rooms | İskele Mah., İnönü Cad. 6 | tel. 0324 8 16 47 51 | www.eserpansiyon. com | Budget*

KAP ANAMUR
The hotel is right on the beach. Friendly owners, pleasant atmosphere. *9 rooms | İskele Mahallesi, Sahil Yolu | tel. 0324 8 14 23 74 | Budget*

MAMURE HOTEL
In Bozyazı in Anamur marina; one of the best average standard hotels in the region. Lovely pool, good restaurant. *42 rooms | Yat Limanı | Bozyazı | 10 km East of Anamur | tel. 0324 8 51 54 00 | www. hotelmamure.com | Expensive*

INSIDER TIP ► YALI MOCAMP
Campsite on the beach, only 3 km (1¾mi) from Anamur, shady grounds, tents and bungalows; easy to reach by taxi. *Tel. 0324 8 14 14 35 | Budget*

INFORMATION

TURIZM DANIŞMA
Atatürk Cad. 64 | tel. 0324 8 14 35 29 | on-line brochure: www.anamur.gen.tr

WHERE TO GO

INSIDER TIP ► KÖŞEKBÜKÜ MAĞARASI ●
This 5400 ft² large stalactite cave is in the mountains around 20 km (12 mi) to the northeast of Anamur. You can do more than just admire the formations here; it is said that the constant temperature of 17° C (63° F) and 80 % humidity is also good for people with asthma and bronchial complaints. *Daily until sunset | entrance fee 3.50 lira | www.anamuronline. com | dolmuş from bus station*

ANTAKYA

(135 E6) (∅ Z7–8) Today's capital (pop. 145,000) of the Hatay Province is, along with Istanbul, one of the oldest cities in Turkey to have been inhabited without interruption.

Antakya, or Antioch in ancient times, was founded by one of Alexander the Great's generals after the victory at Issus in 333 BC; it was a much larger city in the 2nd century BC than it is today. Half a million people lived in the city in those days and

> **WHERE TO START?**
> **Arkeoloji Müzesi:** The archaeological museum on the main square in the new city is a favourite meeting place. All roads branch out from here. The city is divided by the River Orontes; the Old Town is on the other side and that is where St Peter's cave is located.

it was famous for its wealth. It was conquered by the Romans in 60 BC and became the third largest city in the Imperium Romanun after Rome itself and Alexandria. The city was not only the Roman centre of power on the eastern Mediterranean

er in harmony. The narrow oriental old part of Antakya is one of the most beautiful Ottoman city centres in the country. The narrow streets around the *Uzun Çarşı*, the long bazaar, turn a simple stroll into a unique experience.

Magnificent Roman mosaic floor in the museum in Antakya

but also the first centre of Christianity after Jerusalem. It is said that Peter established the first Christian community in a cave here and that it subsequently became the largest of its age under St Paul the Apostle. The ancient city was completely destroyed by several earthquakes. Around 1100 AD the crusaders founded a separate kingdom in Antioch that existed for almost 200 years. After World War I, Antakya was part of the French protectorate of Syria before finally being ceded to Turkey following a referendum held in 1936.

Today, Antakya is one of the most prosperous cities in the whole of Turkey where Moslems, Christians and Jews live togeth-

SIGHTSEEING

ANTAKYA MÜZESI (ARCHAEOLOGICAL MUSEUM) ★

After the museum in Ravenna, this municipal museum has the largest collection of Roman mosaics in the world. The mosaics from the floors and walls are exhibited in five halls. The artworks come mainly from Antioch and Daphne, which was a district where wealthy people had their villas in Roman times, and the port of Seleukia. *Tue–Sun 8.30am–12.30pm, 1.30pm–5.30pm | entrance fee 10 lira | Cumhuriyet Meydanı, Gündüz Cad. 1 (near the main bridge).*

CHURCH OF ST PETER THE APOSTLE ★ ●

The church consists of a portal built in the crusade period through which one enters the cave where, according to the legend, Peter is said to have founded the first community of people who called themselves Christians, only a few years after the death of Jesus. The Vatican declared the site holy in 1983 and it has been a place of pilgrimage since then. A solemn service is held in the cave every year on 29 June, the day of St Peter's death. There is a tunnel that the first Christians used as an escape route at the back of the cave. *Tue–Sun 8am–noon, 1.30pm–4.30pm | entrance fee 10 lira | on the road to Reyhanlı, 1000 m from the centre*

ABDO RESTAURANT

This restaurant serves outstanding Arab food. *Hürriyet Cad. 19/A | tel. 0326 2 12 75 46 | Budget*

INSIDER TIP ANTAKYA EVI RESTAURANT

The Maison d'Antioch serves a large selection of local specialities in its historical rooms. *Silhalı Kuvvetler Cad. 3 | tel. 0326 2 14 13 50 | Moderate*

WHERE TO STAY

There are many hotels in Antakya including boutique hotels in historical buildings. Less expensive accommodation can be found on İstiklal Caddesi.

The Church of St Peter the Apostle in Antakya has always been a place of pilgrimage

FOOD & DRINK

Most of the restaurants in Antakya are located around Hürriyet Caddesi near the river. The cuisine has an Arab influence and many hot spices are used. One speciality is *Çiğ Köfte*, meat balls that are kneaded with hot spices until the meat 'cooks' itself.

INSIDER TIP OTTOMAN PALACE

New five-star hotel with classical, neo-Ottoman furnishings, large pool and wonderful Turkish bath. 10 km (6¼ mi) from the centre. *252 suites | Güngör Uydu Kent | tel. 0326 2 55 16 16 | www. antakyaottomanpalace.com | Moderate–Expensive*

SAVON

The Sehoglus have turned an old soap factory into the most fashionable hotel in town with comfortable rooms, beautiful inner courtyard, bar and restaurant. *40 rooms, 3 suites | Kurtuluş Cad. 192 | tel. 0326 2 14 63 55 | www.savonhotel.com | Expensive*

TURIZM DANIŞMA

Atatürk Cad. | Vali Ürgen Alanı Sok. 47 | tel. 0326 2 16 06 10

WHERE TO GO

ANTIOCHEIA (135 E6) (*Z7*)

An unpaved road turns off towards the fortress 5 km (3 mi) past St Peter's cave on the way to Reyhanli. The castle was built by the Byzantines and later used by the crusaders. Some walls and ramparts are still well-preserved. *15 km (9 mi) from Antakya*

INSIDER TIP HARBIYE/DAPHNE
(135 E6) (*Z8*)

In ancient times, the city that is known as Harbiye today was called Daphne and was the where the wealthy residents of Antakya had their summer homes. The village has a laurel and cypress forest that starts below the main road and stretches for miles past a waterfall and into the plain. According to the Greek legend, this is where the god Apollo tried to seduce Daphne, who out of desperation turned herself into a laurel tree (Turkish: *defne*). Today, the grove is a popular destination for excursions and picnics. There are some restaurants under the shady trees near the waterfall including *Boğaziçi Restaurant (opposite the falls) | tel. 0326 2 31 49 33 | Moderate). 9 km (5½ mi) from Antakya, minibus from bus station or stop a dolmuş on Kurtuluş Caddesi*

SAMANDAĞ
(135 E6) (*Y8*)

Today, Samandağ plays the same role for Antakya as Seleukia did for Antioch in earlier times: the city's port and bathing spot is reached after a journey over the mountains. After travelling a couple of miles to the north towards Çevlik, you reach the ancient harbour city of *Suleukia Pieria*. There are only very few remains to be seen but one impressive example of Roman engineering skill has been preserved. In order to protect the city from floodwater from the mountains, Jewish slaves were forced by Emperor Vespasian and his son to build a canal more than 100 m long that could also serve as a tunnel through the mountain. *25 km (15 mi) southwest of Antakya, dolmuş from bus station*

SILIFKE

(133 D5) (*T7*) Silifke (pop. 52,000) in Mersin Province is a town full of history whose foundation under the name of Seleukia can be traced back to the period of the campaigns of Alexander the Great around 300BC.

Seleukia's importance in ancient times was due to its strategic position at the end of the Göksu valley that broke through the Taurus Mountains to create a gateway to Central Anatolia – the so-called 'Cilician Gate' – to the north of Silifke. Armies from ancient times up to crusaders on their way from Anatolia to Mesopotamia marched through this pass and it is now the main route from the coast to the central Anatolian city of Konya. Emperor Barbarossa drowned in the River Göksu – it was called the Saleph at the time – on 10 June 1190 and this ultimately led to the failure of the third crusade to re-conquer Jerusalem. The castle high above the city is the only witness to Silifke's proud past. The picturesque Old Town nestles against the slope beneath the fortress. The centre, with its fish market and bazaar, is located around *Taşköprü Bridge* built over the Göksu in Roman days.

SIGHTSEEING

ARKEOLOJI MÜZESI (ARCHAEOLOGICAL MUSEUM)

The main attraction in this small museum is its collection of gold coins and silver jewellery from the age of Alexander the Great. *Tue–Sun 9am–5pm | entrance fee 3.50 lira | on the exit road towards Anamur*

AYATEKLA

The place of pilgrimage *(meryemlik)* on the road towards Anamur is named after St Thekla, an early Christian woman who hid from persecution in a cave here. Later, the first Christians used the cave as a secret place of worship until 313 AD. Today,

it has been converted into a subterranean church. *Open daily, you will possibly have to ask the caretaker (bekçi) to let you in | entrance fee 3.75 lira*

SILIFKE KALESI

The Silifke fortress was originally built by Armenian kings and later used by the Knights of St John. The path up to the castle is a pleasant walk through the Old Town. There is a lovely view over Silifke and the delta of the Göksu from the ✂ INSIDER TIP café near the castle.

FOOD & DRINK

There are many traditional *lokantas* in the centre of Silifke. You will find good fish restaurants around 8 km (5 mi) away in Taşucu and in the holiday resort *Kız Kalesi* 25 km (15 mi) to the east.

KALE RESTORAN ✂

The restaurant specialising in meat dishes is located high up on the hill next to the fortress and has good views. *Kalenin Yanı | Moderate*

WHERE TO STAY

CLUB BARBAROSSA

The best hotel in the Kız Kalesi holiday resort has an excellent restaurant – but it can sometimes be rather noisy in the evening. *79 rooms | Kızkalesi-Erdemli | tel. 0324 5 23 23 64 | www.barbarossa.hotel. com | Moderate*

LADES MOTEL

This average standard hotel with a large pool and balconies is closer to Silifke and directly on the seashore. It also organises INSIDER TIP excursions to the bird sanctuary in the Göksu Delta. *22 rooms | tel. 0324 7 41 40 08 | www.ladesmotel.com | Moderate*

LOW BUDGET

▶ You should spend an afternoon between the mosque, church and synagogue on Kurtuluş Avenue in the religious centre of Antakya. The inexpensive *Abdo Restaurant (daily | Hüriyet Caddesi 19/A | tel. 0326 2 12 75 436)* is a good choice for your lunchtime kebab.

▶ The sculptor Abdullah Özalp makes cheap copies of ancient figures in his studio in Antalya. The local museum will 'certify it is a fake' to make it possible for you to export the articles! *Heykeltiras | Karyer Mahellesi | Harbiye Antakya | tel. 0326 2 31 32 88*

INFORMATION

TURIZM DANIŞMA
Veli Gürten Bozbey Caddesi 6 | tel. 0324 714 53 28

WHERE TO GO

INSIDER TIP ▶ CENNET VE CEHENNEM
(133 E5) (𝔐 T7)

Half way between Silifke and Kız Kalesi near Narhkuyu, a road branches off to the Cennet ve Cehennem (Heaven and Hell) Grottos. The lower one of the two large grottos – Hell – is no longer open to visitors today. In ancient times it was believed that this was actually where the gate to hell, guarded by the serpent-headed Typhon, was located. You can reach the entrance to 'Heaven' up 450 stone steps (!) – today, there is a small chapel at its entrance. *Entrance fee 5 lira | 21 km (13 mi) from Silifke*

KIZ KALESI ★
(133 E5) (𝔐 U7)

This holiday resort on the site of ancient Korykos is located opposite the famous *Maiden's Castle (Kız Kalesi)* 300 m from the coast on a small island. According to legend, the daughter of a sultan lived here to be protected from the snakebite that had been prophesised. In spite of these precautions, the maiden was bitten by a snake that had found its way into the castle in a basket of fruit. In Byzantine times, the Maiden's Castle was actually connected to the mainland by a causeway that led across to the castle on the mainland. Some walls of this castle are still standing as are the remains of a chapel inside. A few sarcophaguses from a burial site are the only remains of ancient Korykos to be seen today. *Entrance fee 3.75 lira | 35 km (22 mi) from Silifke | dolmuş or bus from bus station*

The 'Maiden's Castle' on an island off the coast near Silifke

INSIDER TIP ▶ OLBA DIOKAISAREA
(133 D4) (𝔐 T6)

The ancient place of cult worship Diokaisarea with the *Zeus Olbios Temple* – of which 30 early-Corinthian columns are still standing – is located at an altitude of 1100 m (3600 ft) in the uplands of the southern Taurus Mountains near the village of Uzuncaburç to the north of Silifke. The 2300 year old columns point into the sky, surrounded by a few other monuments form the 3rd century BC including the Tyche Temple, in the midst of a beautiful mountain landscape. *Entrance fee 3.75 lira | from Silifke to Uzuncaburç via Demircili, 28 km (17 mi)*

TRIPS & TOURS

The tours are marked in green in the road atlas, pull-out map and on the back cover

1 EXPLORING THE GULF OF GÖKOVA

This tour of the southwestern tip of Turkey includes secluded beaches, lively holiday resorts and ancient sites. 450 km (280 mi); duration: 3–4 days.

You start in **Marmaris → p. 46** and head west towards Datça. After around 10 km (6 mi), the last holiday resorts disappear and a beautiful, fairy-tale stretch through the pine forests of the Datça Peninsula begins. The bends of the serpentine road over the mountains open up unexpected views over the countryside. The first stop

comes after around 25 km (15½mi) where the road branches off to **Bozburun → p. 49** (20 km/12 mi). The fishing village of Bozburun where the *gulets* – the typical boats used for the 'Blue Voyages' – are built is one of the few places in the region to have preserved its original charm. Tuck into a meal of fish at the harbour before setting off back towards Datça along the main road. 10 km (6 mi) after reaching the main road once again, you will be rewarded with a view of the sea. This is the place to make a stop and climb up the nearest hill; the peninsula is so narrow here that you have a ☀ wonderful view of both the Gulf of Gökova in the north

Photo: The harbour bay and fortress in Bodrum

Trips to the sea, into the mountains and in the footsteps of the first Christians, as well as a hike along the Lycian Way

and Hisarönü Gulf to the south. When you arrive at **Datça**, we recommend an overnight stay a little way from the harbour in Old Datça. The next detour takes you to **Knidos**. The 40 km (25 mi) of unsurfaced road to the tip of the peninsula are a challenge for any car. It's more advisable to tackle this section by boat. An outing to the ancient city of Knidos is a very special experience. The ferry to Bodrum, which will take you back to Datça, departs from the small port in **Körmen** on the northern side of the peninsula. When you reach **Bodrum**, you should visit the fortress and stay the night to experience the hustle and bustle of this town on the Aegean *(Manastır Hotel (with a view over the town) | 59 rooms | Kumbahçe Mah. Bariş Sitesi | tel. 0252 3 16 28 58 | www.manastir bodrum.com | Moderate).*

Gümüşlük near Bodrum: restaurants along the shore

Before continuing your journey towards Milas, make a short trip to lovely Gümüşlükan Bay at the western tip of Bodrum Peninsula. Follow the main road towards Turgutreis and, after around 20 km (12 mi), turn off onto the small road towards **Gümüşlük**. This road ends at the sea after around 15 km (9 mi) where there are several pleasant restaurants on the water and a pebble beach which will tempt you to take a dip. Back in Bodrum, head northeast towards **Milas**. The small inland town has a lovely Old Town that is well worth visiting as well as two old notable mosques, *Feruz Bey Camii* (1394) and *Ulu Camii* (1378). After leaving Milas, Route 330 will take you through dense mountain forests to **Yatağan**. Shortly before you arrive, you will pass ancient **Stratonikeia** hidden near the village of Eskihisar. The complex from the 3rd century BC is partially overgrown and now has an enchanted air.

After Yatağan, stay on Route 330 until you reach the regional capital of **Muğla**, the highest point on this trip. When you leave the town, your journey will take you along a breathtaking serpentine road for 30 km (19 mi) until you finally arrive back at the coast once again in Gökova. The small village of **Akyaka** near Gökova is at the tip of the Gulf of Gökova and *Hotel Yücelen (Akyaka Beldesi | Gökova | Moderate)* can be recommended for an overnight stay. You can then take Route 400 from Gökova back to Marmaris.

2 A JOURNEY BACK TO THE ROOTS OF CHRISTIANITY

This excursion takes you through Hatay, the home of Christianity, the crusaders and Armenians that is now characterised by a strong Arab influence. The tour covers around 200 km (125 mi) and takes two days. You start in **Antakya** → p. 86 but before you leave the city to drive down to the coast you should take a step back to the early days of Christianity. St Peter's cave

(Church of St Peter the Apostle) → p. 88 can be found on the road towards Reyhanlı – Süreyya Halefoğlu Caddesi. There are many cave churches throughout Anatolia but this one has an absolutely unique history. It is said that Peter the Apostle founded the first Christian community here a few years after Jesus had been crucified in Jerusalem.

The trip to the coast at Samandağ begins back in the centre of town but before you set off on the 30 km (19 mi) journey you should visit INSIDER TIP Simon Manastırı. The road to the monastery complex around 20 km (12 mi) away is signposted. It was dedicated to St Simon who is said to have lived here for more than 40 years on top of a column. Back on the road to Samandağ, you will pass through terraced hills down to the sea. Samandağ → p. 89 is Antakya's beach. There is an Alevi sanctuary dedicated to the mystic Hızır on a white limestone hill on this beach.

Samandağ is a good place to have a swim and lunch on the beach before heading off to the north and Seleukia Pieria. This is the ancient harbour of Antioch and is significant in Christian teaching as the place from which the Apostle Paul set forth on his missionary journeys. Today, not much of the old port is left. The main attraction is the 130 m-long tunnel that two Roman emperors Vespasian and Titus (father and son) had built by Jewish slaves through the mountain.

Travelling further to the north along the coast road, you reach the village of Çevlik at the foot of Musa Dağ, the setting for Franz Werfel's novel 'The Forty Days of Musa Dagh'. Werfel takes the inhabitants of the villages on Mount Musa to depict the expulsion of the Armenians in the final stages of the Ottoman Empire. Hikes up the mountain can be made from Çevlik. The most difficult 30 km (19 mi) of the trip start after leaving Çevlik. An unsurfaced

road winds its way through the mountains above the cliffs; firstly to the village of Karagöl and then to the ruins of a crusaders' fortress at the tip of Cape Hınzır Burnu. From here, the coast curves to the northeast and the road becomes better as you get closer to the small town of Uluçınar. This is a lovely beach resort and Hotel Aruz (12 rooms | tel. 0326 6 43 24 44 | Moderate) can be recommended for the night. After leaving Uluçınar, the road takes you 30 km (19 mi) towards İskenderun first of all. Turn right, leaving the E91, heading for Belen and Antakya. The road now leads to the pass over the Nuh Mountains where you will be rewarded with a ☀ magnificent panoramic view of the sea and İskenderun just before you reach Belen. Shortly after Belen (10 km/6 mi), there is a small unsurfaced turn-off to the crusaders' fortress of Bagras Kalesi. This castle was an outpost built to protect the route to Antioch in the state founded by the knights while on their first crusade in 1098. Antakya is only 40 km (25 mi) away once you get back on the main road.

3 HIGH MOUNTAINS, COLD LAKES

This tour north of Antalya through the Taurus Mountains to the large lakes in the area is something for nature-lovers and hikers. It covers around 600 km (375 mi), takes 3–4 days and demands a lot of both the car and the driver.

First of all, follow the main road from Antalya → p. 51 to Alanya until you reach Route 685 that turns off to the north shortly before Aksu. The road follows the River Aksu through the mountains and passes two reservoirs in succession, Karaca Ören 1 and 2. Around 10 km (6 mi) after the second reservoir, a small road to the right near the hamlet of Aşağıgökdere will take you to Kovada Gölü a lake in the nature reserve of the same name. Kovada Lake is fed by a natural channel from large Eğirdir Lake. There is a INSIDERTIP lovely hiking trail (3–4 hours) around the lake that should not be missed.

can be rented for overnight stays in the national park. You are also allowed to pitch your tent if you have one with you. The national park is a paradise for hikers and the lake is perfect for swimming and fishing.

The sandy beach at Side with the old city walls as a backdrop

After leaving Lake Kovada, travel north following this watercourse until you reach Eğirdir Gölü from where you will have a fine view of Eğirdir down on the lakeside. Eğirdir is a charming regional town with a historical centre and two islands off shore connected to it via a causeway. *Mavi Göl Oteli (20 rooms | tel. 0246 3116417 | Budget)* on Yeşilada at the tip of the lake is a good, inexpensive place to spend the night. The water in the lake is very clean and perfect for swimming. You leave Eğirdir on the 330 and follow a picturesque route along the lake towards Beyşehir. After around 120 km (75 mi), you arrive in Şarkikaraağaç from where a small road branches off to Kızıldağ National Park on the west shore of Beyşehir Gölü, the third-largest lake in Turkey. There are mountain cabins that

The next day, follow the route along the lake further to the south until you reach Yenişarbademli. The village occupies a site where the Hittites lived 4000 years ago. There is also a Seljuk fortress here directly on the lake. The road now goes 30 km (19 mi) along the lake until you reach a main road (695) near Üstünler. Turn left to Beyşehir where you can explore several Seljuk places of interest and enjoy a good lunch on the lakeside. After a stop in Beyşehir, take the same route back and follow the 695 further to the south. You will be rewarded with 180 km (112 mi) of wonderful mountain road through the Taurus back to the Mediterranean. The 695 meets the main coast road shortly before Manavgat. From here, Side→ p. 76 is only 20 km (12 mi) away on the road to Antalya. Here you can get back into the swing of a tourist resort once again before setting off for Antalya, some 70 km (43 mi) away down the dual carriageway.

4 HIKING THE LYCIAN WAY ●

The Lycian Way is the best-known long-distance hike in Turkey. You do not have to cover the entire distance; you can decide on individual sections or simply make day trips.

The Lycian Way *(Likya Yolu)* leads from Fethiye to Antalya, partly directly along the coast and partly through the Taurus Mountains further inland. It begins a little outside Fethiye in the village of Ovacık and ends shortly before Antalya in Hisarçandır, and covers the magical landscape of ancient Lycia. The trail reaches some of the most charming places on the Mediterranean from Ölüdeniz Bay, the sandy beach at Patara and the sunken cities in Kekova to Olympos National Park. You will find world-famous ancient sites such as Phaselis and Myra or Xanthos and Letoon along the way.

If you want to hike the entire route, you should make sure that you have at least four weeks to do so. The trail is planned for normal hikers and does not demand any particular alpine experience although some stretches are obviously more difficult than others. The trail is divided into 25 sections that can each be hiked in one day. The starting and finishing points and distances are shown on the green-and-yellow signposts on the main roads and in the villages. On the way, trees and rocks are marked with red-and-white stripes. In principle, the entire hiking trail covers the distance from Fethiye to Antalya sometimes below and sometimes above the coastal road so that there are many possibilities to start or stop walking.

However, there are a few stretches in the mountains where you will not come across any large settlements for up to three days. Apart from there, you will almost always be able to find small guesthouses providing bed and breakfast in the villages – at least, in the hiking season. The best times to hike are spring, early summer until mid-June, and then from mid-September until late autumn at the end of November. The first six sections starting in Fethiye → p. 39 take you over the hills or directly along the beach. It does go somewhat up hill and down dale but the difference in altitude does not exceed 500 m. This makes the entire route to Kalkan → p. 58 perfect for not-so-experienced hikers. After Kalkan, the trail leads to Kaş → p. 62 and really goes up into the mountains for the first time; this section is better suited for experienced walkers. This is followed by the stretch between Kaş and Kale (Myra in Antiquity) that is once again quite delightful as – with the exception of a 400 m (1300 ft) high hill – it largely takes you along the sea and is easy walking (stages 12–14). Things get a bit steeper between Kale and Finike where you reach a height of 1700 m (5580 ft) in a karst mountain landscape. This is where you will have to provide for yourself and should be in good physical shape. Finike is followed by an area of lower lying agricultural land that not very interesting; it is best to cross this by bus. However, after that, you will find yourself in Olympos National Park → p. 68; the first sections here down to the wonderful beach resort of Çıralı are also a joy for unexperienced walkers. After Çıralı, you will be faced with the highlands of the national park and the over 2000 m (6500 ft) high Tahtalı Saddle → p. 69. The section from Çıralı to the end of the trail in Hisarçandır should therefore only be tackled by experienced mountain hikers.

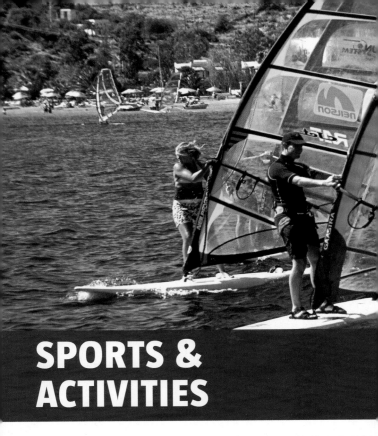

SPORTS & ACTIVITIES

The Turkish Mediterranean coast – this mainly means swimming, diving, sailing and water skiing for active sports enthusiasts.

But in actaul fact, the range of sports on offer along the Turkish coast is in no way restricted to the water. Almost every kind of activity is possible from golf to paragliding and hiking, from trekking and rafting to riding and tennis – the combination of sea and mountains has had a positive effect. In Antalya, it is possible to combine a skiing and beach holiday right up until early summer. Your hotel will assist you in booking activities and, in most cases, also offer tours and special packages.

CANYONING

Canyoning is an adventurous mixture of hiking and climbing in ravines but it requires a certain amount of sporting skill and physical fitness. The best destination for this is the *Saklıkent Gorge* between Fethiye and Kaş. The canyon is so narrow that the sun does not reach the water of the River Eşen at the bottom of the gorge. There is a difference in altitude of no less than 700 m between the two ends of the canyon. *Kesit Tourism (Demircikara Mah Narenciye Cad. 7/4 | Balta Sitesi | Antalya tel. 0242 3 22 44 40 | www.kesit.com)* specialises in tours in the Taurus Mountains.

Thanks to the Taurus Mountains, the choice of sporting activities on the Turkish Mediterranean is not limited to the water

DIVING

There are diving schools in almost every resort. Here are some of the best:

- Alanya | Deep Sea Diving Center | Pal Cafe | Avsallar–Alanya | tel. 0532 2 73 41 36 | www.deep-sea-diving-turkey.de (also in English)

- Antalya | AVCI Diving Hotel Dedeman | tel. 0242 32 79 10 | www.avcidiving.com

- Dalyan | MAVI Diving Center | tel. 0252 2 84 22 51 | www.mavidalis.com.tr

- Datça | Manta Diving Center | Aktur Tatil Sitesi | tel. 0252 7 24 66 54

- Fethiye | European Diving Centre | Kordon Cad., Hukuk Sitesi 20 | tel. 0252 6 14 97 71 | www.europeandivingcentre.com.tr

- Kalkan | DOLPHIN Scuba Team | tel. 0242 8 44 22 42 | www.dolphinscubateam.com

– Kaş | BARAKUDA Club | tel. 0242 8 44 39 55 | www.barakuda-kas.de/index.php?id=2&L=1
– Kemer | MARTI Diving Center | Tekirova Grand Bazaar no. 6 | tel. 0242 8 21 40 70
– Marmaris | Europ. Diving Center | tel. 0252 4 55 47 33 | www.europeandiving centre.com.tr
– Side | Antik Diving Center | Denizbükü Mev. P. K. 14 | tel. 0242 7 53 41 12

GOLF

Golf is becoming increasingly popular on the south coast of Turkey. Many new courses have been laid out around Antalya. *Belek*, a luxurious resort between Antalya and Side, remains the mecca for golf players in the region. *The Gloria Golf Club*; two 18-hole courses (par 72), one 9-hole, 4.9 mi on a 270-acre site *(Acisu Mevkii | tel. 0242 7 15 15 20 | www.gloria.com.tr)* is highly recommendable.

JEEP SAFARIS

Jeep safaris through the Taurus Mountains are available in all major towns on the south coast including Antalya. You can rent a jeep, with or without a driver, or join an organised tour. Children under 8 are not allowed to take part. Meals are served in simple village cafés and you can cool off in mountain streams. *Jeep Safari | Muratpaşa, Tarım Mah., Perge Bulv., Eriş Sitesi, Atalay Apt. 39/2 | Antalya | tel. 0242 3 12 80 66 | www.safariturkey.com*

MOUNTAINBIKING

Bike tours along the coast are becoming all the rage. A wonderful tour for two-wheel fans: ride your bike past thousand-year-old cedar trees on the 45 km (28 mi) route around Kaş. *(Bougainville Travel | İbrahim Serin Cad. 10 | Kaş/Antalya | tel.* 0242 8 36 37 37 | www.bt-turkey.com). Side has also established itself as a fine spot for mountainbike enthusiasts: *Side Nar Travel | Atatürk Bulvarı 118 B | tel. 0242 7 53 34 17 | www.antalyabike.com (with good tour maps).*

PARAGLIDING

Ölüdeniz is one of the best places from which to glide down to the valley below. However, leaping off the 2000 m (6500 ft) high Babadağ is only for the stout-hearted and, of course, you do it at your own risk – there are frequent accidents. *Skysports Paragliding Fethiye | Çarşi Caddesi (ground floor of the Tonoz Hotel) | tel. 0252 6 17 05 11 | www.babadag.com | www.skysports-turkey.com*

RAFTING

There are two rivers on the south coast that are particularly suitable for rafting: *Dalaman* north of Dalyan and *Köprüçay* that can be reached from Antalya. The lower reaches of the *Dalaman* are also not too difficult for beginners. Arrangements can be made in all towns in the region. Organisers drive their guests to the starting point of the 12 km (7½ mi) course (around 75 lira). The best time for rafting on the Köprüçay is Sept/Oct. *Aquarafting Turville | Kırcami Mah., Perge Cad. 95/3 | tel. 0242 3 11 48 45 | www.antalya-rafting.net*

RIDING

INSIDER TIP Riding on the beach at Patara is an unforgettable experience. The sandy beach which is almost 20 km (12 mi) long is often completely deserted and you can gallop past streams and ancient ruins. *(Sultan Han Çiftliği | Patara | tel. 0242 8 43 51 60)*. The *Berke Ranch* is a comfortable place to stay; rides not only for hotel

A unique experience: riding on the beach at Patara

guests *(27 rooms | Hotel Berke Ranch | Akcasaz Mev. Çamyuva | tel. 0242 8 18 03 33 | Expensive)*.

SAILING

The Turkish Mediterranean coast is one of the best sailing regions in Europe. There are large marinas in Marmaris, Bodrum, Fethiye and Antalya. The most popular place from which charter tours depart is Marmaris, from where it is possible to sail along the south coast as well as into the Aegean. See for example: *www.yachtico.com/sailing-area-turkish-riviera-sailing-mediterranean-sea-along-turkish-coast*

SKIING

INSIDER TIP *Saklıkent ski resort* at a height of 1850 m (6070 ft) north of Antalya claims to be closer to the sea and the equator than any other skiing area in the world. The slopes start at altitudes between 2500 m and 2750 m (8200–9000 ft). Accommodation: *Saklıkent Ski Resort (95 Beds | reservations: Hürriyet Bulvarı, Kültür Mah. Dilara Apt., 1st floor, office 14 | Antalya | tel. 0242 4 46 11 37 (-38) | www.*

saklikent.com.tr | Budget–Moderate) and *Saklısale Pension (29 Beds | tel. 0242 4 46 12 00 | Budget)*. The *Bakırlı Café-Restaurant (tel. 0242 4 46 12 80 | Moderate)* and *Sportland Café (tel. 0242 4 46 10 73 | Moderate)* will take care of your hunger. *49 km (30 mi) from Antalya, dolmuş from bus station*

SURFING

Surfing is possible all along the Turkish Riviera between Side and Alanya. More advanced surfers prefer the bays on the southern side of the Datça Peninsula with their excellent wind conditions. *www.surfingatlas.com/country/192*

TREKKING & HIKING

In addition to the Lycian Way, the Taurus Mountains have countless other possibilities for hiking and trekking. Two of the most interesting destinations are Sandras Mountain (2294 m/7526 ft) near Muğla and **INSIDER TIP** *Butterfly Valley* with its millions of beautiful butterflies at the foot of Babadağ near Fethiye; however, its entrance can only be reached from the sea *(boats from Ölüdeniz | www.infethiye.net)*.

TRAVEL WITH KIDS

Turkey is a country that loves children and where they have always simply been part of everyday life. It is a matter of course to travel with youngsters here. You can visit any restaurant with children and you'll often find that the waiters will take care of the children to let you eat your meal in peace.

The same applies to hotels. The large holiday complexes have mini-clubs for the little ones with trained staff to provide all kinds of activities and fun things to do. This will keep the youngsters happy and gives parents the chance to spend an afternoon relaxing in the sun by themselves. Some hotels cater especially for families with children and offer special tennis, swimming and surfing courses.

But even if you don't book into a holiday resort that is especially geared to children, is anything more fun than spending a day on the beach armed with a bucket and spade?

You can always visit the national parks and museums as well. Many national parks in the Taurus Mountains offer a combination of scenic highlights and interesting historical sites. The *Termessos National Park* near Antalya is a wonderful place to go for a walk and explore ancient monuments set off against a magnificent natural backdrop.

Children are always welcome in Turkey – and many little ones are perfectly happy just playing around on the beach with a bucket and spade

The large *museum in Antalya* has long since adapted its programme of events to cater to children. In addition to traditional holiday pastimes, there are more and more commercial enterprises specially devoted to children of all ages in the main tourist centres. *Water adventure parks* where children can have fun on giant slides have become exceedingly popular.

However you should bear one thing in mind: not all hotel pools have lifeguards – especially at night. There is often no grate over the pool's drain which can be especially dangerous for small children. And you should avoid letting children eat food which quickly 'goes off', such as mayonnaise, cream, fish or chicken on hot days when the temperature can reach more than 30° C (86° F).

afternoon. The tour usually ends with a barbeque. You can hire canoes and life jackets from various agencies in Patara *(around 50 lira per person incl. barbeque)*. *Dardanos Turizm (tel. 0242 843 51 09)* and *Nikola's Tour (tel. 0242 8 43 51 54)*

ANTALYA – LYCIAN COAST

ANTALYA MÜZESI
(128 B6) *(ɰ K5–6)*

There is a special section for children in the Antalya Museum (to the right after the entrance). It is the first of its kind in a Turkish museum and has a display of toys, pretty money boxes and many other things. Youngsters can help restore small objects in the INSIDER TIP children's workshop or take a course in pottery making and painting. *Tue–Sun Oct–April 8.30am–12.30pm, 1.30pm–5.30pm, May–Sept 9am–6pm | entrance fee 7.50 lira | Konyaaltı Cad. | tel. 0242 2 38 56 88 | www. antalyamuzesi.gov.tr/en*

INSIDER TIP AQUAPARK DEDEMAN
(128 B6) *(ɰ K6)*

This water adventure park extending over some 10 acres under the roof of the Hotel Dedeman is located about 3 km (2 mi) from the centre of Antalya on the way to Lara Beach. Gigantic pools and slides, baby park, cafés, restaurants – and all this on a slope with a splendid view of the sea. Not only for children! *May–mid-Sept daily 10am–5pm | Dedeman Oteli | Şirinyalı Mah., Lara Yolu 1 | tel. 0242 3 16 44 00 | www.aquaparkantalya.com.tr | entrance fee 45 lira, children 25 lira; free for the under 7s and over 60s*

AQUAWORLD KEMER
(127 E4–5) *(ɰ J6)*

Heaven on earth for young and young-at-heart water fans in the middle of town: enormous slides – the names 'Kamikaze'

There are lots of children in Turkey – and they love to meet others

THE SOUTHWEST

CANOE TOUR ON THE EŞEN
(126 A–B 5–6) *(ɰ F6–7)*

A canoe or paddle tour on the River Eşen is a special treat for all the family. In contrast to rafting, this is not very strenuous and not at all dangerous for children. The Eşen emerges from the Taurus Mountains north of the large beach at Patara where it flows across the sand into the sea. The tours begin at around 11am under the bridge in Kınık. After about 6 hours – including breaks for swimming and lunch – you reach the beach at Patara in the late

and 'Crazy River' give you a good idea of what they are like – and a huge pool make sure you will have fun all day long. If the children are old enough to take care of themselves, mum and dad can relax in the spa. Please note: don't underestimate the strength of the sun even when you are in the water! *May–Oct, daily 9am–11pm | Deniz Caddesi | Kemer | tel. 0242 8 14 58 23 | entrance fee 25 lira, children over 7: 12.50 lira*

CAVE TOUR

A tour of the caves around Antalya is fascinating for not-so-young children. There are around 500 caves in the limestone Taurus Mountains but not all are accessible to visitors. The largest and most interesting is *Karain Cave* on the road to Burdur (27 km/17 mi northwest of Antalya) (128 B5) *(ᗕ J5)*. It was discovered by the Italian Giuseppe Moretti during World War I and traces of human existence have been found dating back as far as 50,000 years. The objects found during excavations carried out since 1946 include spearheads and pieces of skeletons and are on display in the local museum. *Beldibi Cave*, around 30 km (19 mi) southwest of Antalya (127 E4) *(ᗕ J6)*, also has traces our ancestors from Paleolithic times left behind in the form of wall paintings. Legend has it that some soldiers fled to *Damlataş Cave* near Alanya (131 D4) *(ᗕ N6)* to escape gas attacks during World War II. Some were asthmatics and felt the cave had done them good; today, the cave is a place where people with breathing difficulties come for treatment. *With the exception of Damlataş Cave, you will need a hire car to get there*

PARK BOWLING
(128 B6) *(ᗕ K6)*

For youngsters who are easily bored: one of the best and largest bowling alleys in all of Turkey can be found in Antalya not far from Lara beach – 16,150 ft² of fun with 10 lanes. In addition, there are around 60 electronic game consoles and nine billiard tables. *Daily 10am–11pm | Şirinyalı Mah. | Lara Yolu | Park Oteli Altı | Antalya | tel. 0242 3 16 44 09 10 | www.depark.com.tr*

TURKISH RIVIERA

ALANYA PIRATE CASTLE
(131 D4) *(ᗕ N6–7)*

The fortress on the hill in Alanya makes an exciting excursion, especially for older children. Once they reach the top of the hill, they can enjoy clambering all over the old walls and ramparts. *Daily 8am–7pm | entrance fee 12 lira | www.alanya-site.com/alanya_castle.html*

There is so much to discover snorkelling

FESTIVALS & EVENTS

There are major culture and music festivals in the tourist hotspots of Marmaris, Fethiye and Antalya throughout the summer and autumn, while the towns and villages further inland invite you to take part in their traditional celebrations.

PUBLIC HOLIDAYS

1 Jan *Yılbaşı* (New Year's Day), **23 April** *Ulusal Egemenlik ve Çocuk Bayramı* (Festival of National Sovereignty and Children), **1 May** *Birlik ve Dayanısma Günü* (Day of Unity and Solidarity), **19 May** *Gençlik ve Spor Bayramı* (Day of Youth and Sport), **30 Aug** *Zafer Bayramı* (Victory Celebration, end of the War of Independence 1922), **29 Oct** *Cumhuriyet Bayramı* (Foundation Day of the Turkish Republic 1923)

RELIGIOUS HOLIDAYS

In the Islamic lunar calendar, holidays move back 11 days every year: **25–28 Oct 2012/ 15–18 Oct 2013/4–7 Oct 2014** *Kurban Bayramı*, the highest Islamic feast lasts four days; **20 July 2012/9 July 2013/28 June 2014** Start of *Ramadan*; **19–21 Aug 2012/**

8–10 Aug 2013/28–30 July 2014 3-day *Sugar Feast* at the end of Ramadan

FESTIVALS & EVENTS

JANUARY
▶ *Camel fights:* colourfully dressed camels attempt to get the better of each other in Kale near Kaş

APRIL
▶ *Easter mass* in Antakya
▶ *Kite Festival:* dazzling kites rise in the air on the Datça Peninsula to celebrate the Turkish children's festival on 23/24 April

MAY
▶ *Regattas* and supporting programme in Marmaris

JUNE
▶ ★ *Aspendos Opera and Ballet Festival.* International and Turkish ensembles breathe new life into the magnificent Roman amphitheatre
▶ INSIDERTIP *Mass in the Church of St Peter the Apostle:* solemn mass in the cave church in Antakya on 29 June

Whether it is a summer festival for tourists or something completely traditional: celebrations are held here all year round

JULY
▶ *Caretta Caretta Festival:* music and cultural festival in honour of the logger-head turtles in Dalyan (1–3 July)
▶ *Antakya Culture Festival:* singing and dancing in Hatay (Antakya) (20–23 July)
▶ *Manavgat Culture Festival:* concerts and dances near the waterfalls, on the beach, and in the town (23–27 July)

AUGUST
▶ *Karakucak Wrestling Championship:* in Adana, in the Taurus Mountains on the last Sunday in August
▶ *Almond Harvest:* harvest festival on the Datça Peninsula (18–21 August)

SEPTEMBER
▶ *Bullfights* in Ula/Muğla (8/9)
▶ *Theatre and concerts* in front of the Temple of Apollo in Side, 2 weeks from mid-September

▶ *International Tango Festival* in Marmaris (16–21 Sept)

OCTOBER
▶ *Golden Orange Film Festival:* film festival in Antalya with the latest international and Turkish films
Three-day ▶ *Regatta* of the *gulet* wooden boats from Bodrum to Marmaris (from 24 Oct)
▶ INSIDER TIP *Paragliding Festival:* gliders from all over the world float down from Babadağ to the beach or into the water in Ölüdeniz/Fethiye (5 days starting on 18 Oct)

DECEMBER
Father Christmas visits Kale/Myre on 5/6 December and takes part in the ecumenical ▶ *services* in St Nicholas' Church.
▶ *Christmas mass* in Antakya especially the Church of St Peter the Apostle

LINKS, BLOGS, APPS & MORE

LINKS

▶ www.kultur.gov.tr/EN The Ministry of Culture and Tourism's extensive site with a detailed history of the country and its archaeology as well as in-depth information on towns and cities, including those on the south coast. Includes virtual tours of all sorts of museums and towns

▶ www.hotelguide.com.tr The ultimate Turkish hotel portal provides a detailed search mask and a great deal of information about special offers in each region.

▶ www.antalya-web.com This travel and information portal covers virtually everything that you may want to know before setting off on holiday – and not just on Antalya but on other places to visit as well

▶ www.lycianturkey.com This part of Turkey was home to the ancient Lycians – one of the most enigmatic people of Antiquity who were culturally distinct from the rest of the ancient world. Around twenty major sites remain today with the Lycians' unusual funerary architecture dominating this breathtakingly unspoiled area.

▶ www.justlanded.com/english/Turkey Informative website about everyday living in Turkey for anyone living, working or studying there, covering topics such as visas, housing, jobs and finance. And if you need more details, get in touch with the 'Just Landed Community'

BLOGS & FORUMS

▶ www.facebook.com/pages/Lycian-Way-Blog/113530168727527 See what others have written about the Lycian Way, with tips and photos.

▶ www.travelpod.com/travel-blog-city/Turkey/Turkish%20Riviera/tpod.html Travel blogs on the Turkish Riviera including a report on a 'Blue Voyage' and other cruises

Regardless of whether you are still preparing your trip or already on the south coast of turkey: these addresses will provide you with more information, videos and networks to make your holiday even more enjoyable

▶ www.blogexpat.com/en/dir/turkey/blog/ Ranging from 'The Adventures of an American in Antalya' to photography and travel blogs with a focus on ancient and sacred sites, find out more about the south coast of Turkey and the country in general from those who live there

BLOGS & FORUMS

▶ wn.com/hiddendatca Four short films about Datça, the old city centre and the excavations in Knidos over the years

▶ www.5min.com/Video/Visit-Alanya-in-the-Turkish-Riviera-255972229 Video in English focussing on Alanya and with links to other similar videos

▶ www.cirali.org/en This web portal with useful information and addresses on Çıralı/Olympos also has some fascinating facts about seas turtles and a film on 'The Turtles and Tourists'

VIDEOS

▶ Turkey's Mediterranean Coast English language app with travel information: maps, planning, safety, health, addresses

▶ Cruising the Mediterranean App for people on a cruise as well as yachtsmen. Information on all cruise ships active in the Mediterranean, sailing routes, ports and their infrastructure, as well as shore visits

APPS

▶ www.tripwolf.com Things to do and what to see on the South Coast in Turkey: travel tips, photos, blogs and evaluations by community members

▶ www.lonelyplanet.com/thorntree Forum not only for tourist travel but also with information on work possibilities. Post your own evaluations, photos and reports

NETWORK

TRAVEL TIPS

ARRIVAL

✈ Most holiday-makers arrive by plane. You can reach any airport in Turkey, either directly or with a stopover in Istanbul, with Turkish Airlines *(www.turkish airlines.com)* as well as other major airlines including British Airways *(www.british airways.com)* and budget operators such as easyJet *(www.easyjet.com)*. There are non-stop charter flights throughout the year to Istanbul, Izmir and Antalya, as well as to Dalaman and Bodrum in the high season. The cost of flights varies considerably depending on the season and destination: it is worth spending some time comparing prices or consult your local travel agent.

🚗 If you intend to drive, plan your route carefully and inform yourself about the countries you have to pass through, customs formalities and other regulations. Motoring organisations may be able to help. You can drive via Croatia and Serbia, but it is more advisable to take the Hungary-Romania route – or drive to Italy and cross to Turkey by ferry (see below).

🚆 Trains depart from London for Istanbul every day except Christmas Day. The London-Istanbul train journey may cost much more than an air fare, but it is a 3-day adventure, during which you can rediscover some of the mystery and romance of long-distance sleeping-car travel across Europe.

🚢 If you have enough time, a trip by ferry from Venice or Brindisi can be a pleasant alternative. The journey from Venice to Izmir takes around two and a half days and costs from around 330 pounds/510 US dollars (incl. car transport); from Brindisi one and a half days and around 250 pounds/380 US dollars. *www.ankertravel.com | www.feribot.net*

RESPONSIBLE TRAVEL

It doesn't take a lot to be environmentally friendly whilst travelling. Don't just think about your carbon footprint whilst flying to and from your holiday destination but also about how you can protect nature and culture abroad. As a tourist it is especially important to respect nature, look out for local products, cycle instead of driving, save water and much more. If you would like to find out more about eco-tourism please visit: *www.ecotourism.org*

BANKS & MONEY

Banks are usually open from 9am–noon and from 1pm–5pm. Branches with the *Öğlen Açık* sign do not close for lunch and branches in shopping centres often have longer opening hours. Almost all banks have cash dispensers and you can withdraw money around the clock with your EC or credit card; HSBC Bank machines also issue euro notes. If you need to exchange money, go to one of the special exchange offices *(döviz bürosu)* where you will receive a better rate than at a bank. Do not exchange money before you leave home – the rate is always lower than in Turkey. Pounds and euros are accepted almost everywhere in larger centres.

From arrival to weather

Holiday from start to finish: the most important addresses and information for your trip to the south coast of Turkey

BUSES

Buses are still the most common way of getting around in Turkey. There is a bus terminal (*garaj* or *otogar*) in every town and village and buses travel to even the most remote corners of the country. To minimise the risk of being involved in an accident, it is a good idea to select one of the more renowned companies such as *Ulusoy (www.ulsoy.com.tr)* or *Varan (www.varan.com.tr)*.

CAMPING

The best campsites are the state-run 'Forest Camps' *(Orman Kampı)* supervised by the Ministry of Forestry. They can generally be found in shady woodland and have good facilities including telephone, kiosk and shop, places to cook, a laundry, showers with hot water and wastewater disposal for motorhomes and caravans. *www.camping.info*

GÖKOVA ORMAN KAMPI

(125 D4) *(ᗢ D5)* In the beautiful bay of Akyaka; very shady. Capacity: 300 tents and 70 caravans. *Akyaka Köyü | Gökova | tel. 0252 2 46 50 35 | June–Aug*

KATRANCI ORMAN KAMPI

(125 E6) *(ᗢ F6)* Under trees, on the sea approx. 10 km (6 mi) from Fethiye. *Fethiye-Muğla Yolu | Katrancı | tel. 0252 4 63 64 06 | June–Oct*

KINDILÇEŞME ORMAN KAMPI

(127 E5) *(ᗢ J7)* On Olympos Beach in Beydağları National Park, shady. *Beydağları (Olympos) Milli Parkı | Kemer | tel. 0242 8 14 10 75 | closed Jan*

BUDGETING

Coffee	3.50 lira
	for a cup of Nescafe
Snack	4 lira
	for a döner kebab
Simit	80 kuruş
	for a sesame crescent
Beer	6 lira
	for a bottle of beer in a restaurant
Petrol	3.50 lira
	for one litre of super
Hamam	60 lira
	for per visit, including massage, etc.

CAR HIRE

Hire prices start at around 100 lira (per day, incl. full insurance, unlimited mileage). It is often more economical to reserve a car from home. Rent-a-car in Antalya: *AVIS | tel. 0242 2 41 66 93 | www.avis.com.tr; Budget | tel. 0242 2 43 30 06 | www.trbudget.com*. There are small agencies with cheap offers on almost every corner in the Old Town.

CURRENCY

The unit of currency is the Turkish lira (TRY). There are 200, 100, 50, 20, 10 and 5 lira notes as well as 1 lira and 50, 25 and 10 kuruş coins.

CUSTOMS

There is no limit to the amount of Turkish and foreign currency that can be brought

CURRENCY CONVERTER

£	TRY	TRY	£
1	2.80	1	0.35
3	8.40	3	1.05
5	14	5	1.75
13	36.40	13	4.55
40	112	40	14
75	210	75	26
120	335	120	42
250	700	250	87.50
500	1400	500	175

$	TRY	TRY	$
1	2	1	0.50
3	6	3	1.50
5	10	5	2.50
13	26	13	6.50
40	80	40	20
75	150	75	37.50
120	240	120	60
250	500	250	125
500	1000	500	250

For current exchange rates see www.xe.com

into the country. However, you must present a receipt for any carpets or other articles of value purchased in Turkey. Be careful about buying genuine antiques: as a rule, items that are more than 100 years old can not be exported. And it is strictly forbidden to take ancient stones and other antiques out of the country. This also applies to fossils. Even articles that you bought cheaply from a street trader can cause enormous problems.

DOLMUŞ

Travelling by shared taxi, dolmuş (pronounced: dolmoosh) is economical; usually around one third of the price of a taxi. These small buses or large taxis travel on specific routes in the towns and surrounding countryside and stop any where to pick up or drop passengers. Tell the driver where you want to go and ask the fare.

DRIVING

To enter the country by car, you need your driving license, registration papers and a green insurance card. The details of the car will be entered into your passport – be sure that this is removed when you leave the country. Speed limits: in built-up areas 50 kph; outside 90 kph; on motorways 120 kph. It is compulsory to wear seatbelts and there is a total ban on driving after you have consumed alcohol. Information and maps from the Turkish Touring and Automobile Club (TTOK), Istanbul | tel. 0212 2 82 81 40).

ELECTRICITY

The current in Turkey is 220 volt AC. Power failures occur occasionally in more remote districts so it is always a good idea to have a torch with you.

EMBASSIES & CONSULATES

BRITISH EMBASSY
Şehit Ersan Caddesi 46/A | Çankaya, Ankara | tel. 0312-455 3344 | ukinturkey. fco.gov.uk/en

BRITISH VICE-CONSULATE ANTALYA
Gürsu Mahallesi | 324. Sokak No:6, Konyaaltı, Antalya | tel. 0242 228 28 11 | ukinturkey.fco.gov.uk/en

US EMBASSY ANKARA
110 Atatürk Blvd. | Kavaklıdere 06100, Ankara | tel. 0312-455-5555 | turkey.us embassy.gov

US CONSULATE ADANA

Girne Bulvari No: 212 Guzelevler Mah. Yüregir | Adana | tel. 0322 346 62 62 | adana.usconsulate.gov

CANADIAN EMBASSY ANKARA

Cinnah Caddesi no: 58 | 06690, Cankaya | Ankara | tel.: 0312 409 27 00 | www.canada international.gc.ca/turkey-turquie

CANADIAN CONSULATE ISTANBUL

209 Buyukdere Caddesi | Tekfen Tower, 16th Floor | Levent 4, Istanbul | tel. 0212 385 97 00 | www.canadainternational. gc.ca/turkey-turquie

Other embasies and consulates can be found under *embassy.goabroad.com/ embassies-in/turkey*

EMERGENCY SERVICES

Police: *tel. 155*; fire brigade: *tel. 110*; doctor: *tel. 112*

HEALTH

Tap water in Turkey – especially in the large cities – is not suitable for drinking. Take a bottle of mineral water with you to your hotel room.
You will be treated free of charge in state hospitals (SSK) and health offices *(saĝlik ocaĝi)* if you have international health insurance. However, it is less compli- cated and more convenient to take out travel insurance before you leave home; private clinics are usually better equipped. Normal medicines are usually less ex- pensive in chemist's *(eczane)* than in the UK.
A comprehensive list of hospitals and doctors in the region can be found on the British Embassy website *(ukinturkey. fco.gov.uk/en)* under Antalya/Adana

INTERHOSPITAL ANTALYA

Kızıltoprak Mah | Meydan PTT Arkası | 933 Sok | tel: 0311 1500

IMMIGRATION

A multiple-entry, sticker-type visa, valid for three months, can be obtained at any point of entry into Turkey for a fee: UK citizens: £10 (Important: Payments in pounds must be in Bank of England £10 notes only. No Scottish or Northern Irish notes and no other values of notes, i.e. £5 or £20); US citizens: US$20; Canadian citizens: US$60. *More Information: www. mfa.gov.tr/consular-info.en.mfa*

INFORMATION

TURKISH CULTURE & TOURISM OFFICE

Fourth Floor | 29–30 St James's Street | London SW1A 1HB | tel: 020 78397778 | www.gototurkey.co.uk

2525 Massachusetts Ave. | Washington, DC 20008 | tel: (202) 612-6800 | 821 United Nations Plaza | New York, NY 10017 | tel: (212) 687-2194 | tourismturkeysite.com

INTERNET

There are several Internet providers in Turkey but the state-operated Türk Telekom *(www.ttnet.com.tr)* and private Super- online *(www.superonline.com)* are the largest and best. Ask you provider if you will also have net access in Turkey. Almost all hotels offer free ADSL and Wi-Fi in the rooms or at least in the lobby. There are many informative websites with informa- tion on Turkey on the Internet:
www.kulturturizm.gov.tr – Information site of the Turkish Ministry of Culture and Tourism, also in English
www.biletix.com.tr – Tickets for events at your destination can be bought in advance

Kaleköy near Kaş overlooked
by the Byzantine castle

www.aytport.com – Site of Antalya Airport
with departure and landing times

INTERNET CAFÉS

There are Internet cafés in every city in
Turkey. One hour costs between 2.50–
6 lira.

– *Antalya: Greenpoint Internetcafé | Güllük
Cad. Çankaya 2 | Kat 2/5 | tel. 0242
2 44 49 84 | greenpoint@aidata.com.tr;
Nexus Internet Café | Atatürk Cad., Akbaba
Pasaj 79/4 | tel. 0242 2 44 35 76 | nexus07
@yahoo.com*
– *Fethiye: Line Café | Cumhuriyet Mah. Yalı
Sok. 5B | tel. 0252 6 12 71 55 | linecafe@
hotmail.com*

– *Kaş: Bougainville Travel Internet Corner |
Çukurbağlı Cad. | tel. 0242 8 36 37 37 |
info@bougainville-turkey.com*
– *Marmaris: Marmaris Internet Café | Köylü
Pazarı Karşısı | Yat Limanı (at the marina) |
tel. 0252 4 13 72 37 | cafe@marmariscafe.
com.tr*
– *Side: Side Internet Center | Leylak City |
near Hotel Köseoğlu | tel. 0242 7 53 23 98 |
cafe@sideinternet.com*

PHONES & MOBILE PHONES

You need prepaid cards that can be purchased in post offices and at kiosks to be
able to use the *Türk Telekom* phone boxes.
International calls are considerably less
expensive if you use the *TT Kart* (5, 10 or
25 lira).

Dialling code for the UK: 0044; for the
US 001. The dialing code for Turkey from
the UK is 0090; from the USA 01190.
Mobile phones are very common in Turkey
and the network is extensively developed.
Mobile phones from abroad are subject
to roaming charges and these can be expensive. For incoming calls, you may be
charged for half of the call.

PHOTOGRAPHY

It is generally forbidden to take photo-
graphs of military personnel and complexes. You should also not take photos
of veiled women and it is sensible to leave
your camera in its case when you are in
conservative districts.

POST

The post is called the PTT and offices are
usually open from 8am–5pm on week-
days. Main post offices are also often
open until later. International postage for
cards and letters costs 1.10 lira to most
countries.

TAXI

Travelling by taxi is relatively inexpensive but make sure that the meter is turned on. During the day, you will see *günduz* and *gece* after midnight; the night tariff (until 6am) is 50 percent higher. The basic charge is lower in cities than in small towns. In some cities, taxi drivers are authorised to charge 50% extra for trips to the airport.

TIME

Turkey is one hour ahead of Central European Time and 2 hours ahead of GMT. The same applies in daylight saving periods which are the same in Turkey as in the rest of Europe.

TIPPING

Tips (around 10 percent) are usual – and expected – in hotels and restaurants but not in taxis.

WEATHER & CLIMATE

On the coast, the high season lasts from the beginning of May to the end of October but it is still possible to swim in Nov/Dec. It can be very hot in July and August and sometimes there are torrential downpours all along the coast in the winter months.

WEATHER IN ANTALYA

	Jan	Feb	March	April	May	June	July	Aug	Sept	Oct	Nov	Dec
Daytime temperatures in °C/°F	15/59	16/61	18/64	21/70	25/77	30/86	34/93	34/93	31/88	26/79	21/70	17/63
Nighttime temperatures in °C/°F	6/43	7/45	8/46	11/52	15/59	19/66	23/73	23/73	19/66	15/59	11/52	8/46
Sunshine hours/day	5	5	7	8	10	12	12	12	10	8	7	5
Precipitation days/month	11	9	6	4	3	1	0	0	1	4	5	11
Water temperatures in °C/°F	16/61	16/61	16/61	17/63	20/68	23/73	25/77	27/81	26/79	23/73	20/68	18/64

USEFUL PHRASES TURKISH

PRONUNCIATION

ı	like 'a' in 'ago', e.g.: ırmak
c	like 'j' in 'jump', e.g.: cam
ç	like 'ch' in 'chat', e.g.: çan
h	like English 'h', or 'ch' in Scottish 'loch', e.g.: hamam
ğ	a silent letter than extends the vowel before it, e.g.: yağmur
j	like 's' in 'leisure', e.g.: jilet
ş	like 'sh' in 'ship', e.g.: teker
v	like 'v' in 'violin', e.g.: vermek
y	like 'y' in 'young', e.g.: yok
z	like 'z' in 'zoom', e.g.: deniz

IN BRIEF

Yes/No/Maybe	Evet/Hayır/Belki
Please/Thank you	Lütfen/Teşekkür (ederim) or Mersi
Excuse me, please!	Afedersin/ Afedersiniz
May I ...?	İzin verir misiniz?
Pardon?	Efendim? Nasıl?
I would like to .../Have you got ...?	... istiyorum/... var mı?
How much is ...?	... ne kadar? Fiyatı ne?
I (don't) like that	Beğendim/Beğenmedim
good/bad	iyi/kötü
broken/doesn't work	bozuk/çalışmıyor
too much/much/little	çok fazla/çok/ az
all/nothing	hepsi/hiç
Help!/Attention!/Caution!	İmdat!/Dikkat!/Aman!
ambulance	ambulans
police/fire brigade	polis/itfaiye
Prohibition/forbidden	yasak/ yasak

GREETINGS, FAREWELL

Good morning!/afternoon!/ evening!/night!	Günaydın/İyi Günler!/ İyi Akşamlar!/İyi Geceler!
Hello! / Goodbye!	Merhaba!/Allaha ısmarladık!
See you	Hoşçakal (plural: Hoşçakalın)/ Bye bye!

Türkçe biliyormusun?

"Do you speak Turkish?" This guide will help you to say the basic words and phrases in Turkish.

DATE & TIME

Monday/Tuesday/Wednesday	Pazartesi/Salı/Çarşamba
Thursday/Friday/Saturday	Perşembe/Cuma/Cumartesi
Sunday/working day	Pazar/İş günü
Holiday	Tatil Günü/Bayram
today/tomorrow/yesterday	bugün/yarın/dün
hour/minute	saat/dakika
day/night/week	gün/gece/hafta
month/year	ay/yıl
What time is it?	Saat kaç?

TRAVEL

open/closed	açık/kapalı
departure/arrival	kalkış/varış
toilets / ladies/gentlemen	tuvalet (WC) / bayan/bay
Where is ...?/Where are ...?	Nerede ...?/ neredeler ...?
left/right	sol/sağ
straight ahead/back	ileri/geri
close/far	yakın/uzak
bus/tram/underground / taxi/cab	otobüs/tramvay/metro / taksi
bus stop/cab stand	durak/taksi durağı
parking lot/parking garage	park yeri/otopark
train station/harbour/airport	istasyon/liman/havaalanı
schedule/ticket	tarife/bilet
single/return	tek gidiş/gidiş dönüş
train/track	tren/peron
I would like to rent ...	... kiralamak istiyorum
a car	bir otomobil/araba
a boat/rowing boat	bir tekne/sandal
petrol/gas station	benzin istasyonu
petrol/gas / diesel	benzin/dizel
leaded/unleaded	kurşunlu/kurşunsuz
breakdown/repair shop	arıza/tamirhane

FOOD & DRINK

Could you please book a table for tonight for four?	Lütfen bize bu akşama dört kişilik bir masa ayırın.
on the terrace/by the window	terasta/pencere kenarında
The menu, please	menü lütfen

Could I please have ...?	... alabilir miyim lütfen?
bottle/carafe/glass	şişe/karaf/bardak
knife/fork/spoon	bıçak/çatal/kaşık
salt/pepper/sugar/vinegar/oil	tuz/karabiber/şeker/sirke/zeytinyağı
milk/cream/lemon	süt/kaymak/limon
cold/too salty/not cooked	soğuk/fazla tuzlu/pişmemiş
with/without ice	buzlu/buzsuz
Water sparkling/still	su/soda
vegetarian/allergy	vejetaryan/alerji
May I have the bill, lease?	Hesap lütfen
bill/receipt/tip	fatura/fiş/bahşiş

SHOPPING

Where can I find...?	... nerede bulurum?
I'd like .../I'm looking for ...	... istiyorum/... arıyorum
Do you put photos onto CD?	CD'ye fotoğraf basıyor musnuz?
pharmacy/chemist	eczane/parfümeri
baker/market	fırın/pazar
shopping centre/department store	alışveriş merkezi/bonmarşe
grocery/supermarket	gıda marketi, bakkal/süpermarket
100 grammes/1 kilo	yüz gram/bir kilo
expensive/cheap/price	pahalı/ucuz/fiyat
more/less	daha çok/daha az

ACCOMMODATION

I have booked a room	Bir oda rezervasyonum var
Do you have any ... left?	Daha ... var mı?
Single bed/single room	tek yataklı/tek kişilik oda
Double bed/double room	çift yataklı/çift kişilik oda
breakfast/half board	kahvaltı/yarım pansiyon/
full board (American plan)	tam pansiyon
at the front/seafront	ön tarafta/denize bakan
shower/sit-down bath	duş/banyo
key/room card	anahtar/oda kartı
luggage/suitcase/bag	bagaj/bavul/çanta

BANKS, MONEY & CREDIT CARDS

bank/ATM	banka/ATM
pin code	şifre
I'd like to change ...	... bozduracağım
cash/credit card	nakit/kredi kartı
bill/coin	banknot/demir para
change	bozuk para

USEFUL PHRASES

HEALTH

doctor/dentist/paediatrician	doktor/diş doktoru/çocuk doktoru
hospital/emergency clinic	hastane/acil doktor
fever/pain	ateş/ağrı
diarrhoea/nausea/sunburn	ishal/bulantı/güneş yanığı
inflamed/injured	iltihaplı/yaralı
plaster/bandage	yara bandı/gazlı bez
ointment/cream	merhem/krem
pain reliever/tablet	ağrı kesici/hap

POST, TELECOMMUNICATIONS & MEDIA

stamp/postcard/letter	posta pulu/kartpostal/mektup
I need a phone card	Bir telefon kartı lazım
I'm looking for a prepaid card	Bir hazırkart lazım
Where can I find internet access?	İnternete nereden girebilirim?
dial/connection/engaged	çevirmek/hat/meşgul
socket/adapter/charger	priz/adaptör/şarj aleti
computer/battery/rechargeable battery	bilgisayar/pil/akü
internet connection/wifi	internet bağlantısı/wireless
e-mail/file/print	(e-)mail (e-posta)/dosya/basmak

LEISURE, SPORTS & BEACH

beach/bathing beach	sahil/plaj
sunshade/lounger	(güneş) şemsiye(si)/şezlong
low tide/high tide/current	med/cezir/akıntı

NUMBERS

0	sıfır	15	on beş
1	bir	16	on altı
2	iki	17	on yedi
3	üç	18	on sekiz
4	dört	19	on dokuz
5	beş	20	yirmi
6	altı	21	yirmi bir
7	yedi	50	elli
8	sekiz	100	yüz
9	dokuz	200	iki yüz
10	on	1000	bin
11	onbir	2000	iki bin
12	oniki	10000	on bin
13	on üç	½	yarım
14	on dört	¼	çeyrek

NOTES

ROAD ATLAS

The green line ▬▬▬ indicates the Trips & tours (p. 92–97)
The blue line ▬▬▬ indicates the Perfect route (p. 30–31)

All tours are also marked on the pull-out map

Photo: near Aspendos

Exploring the South Coast of Turkey

The map on the back cover shows how the area has been sub-divided

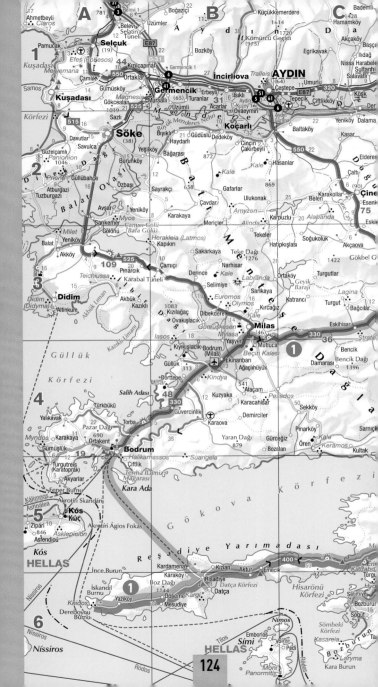

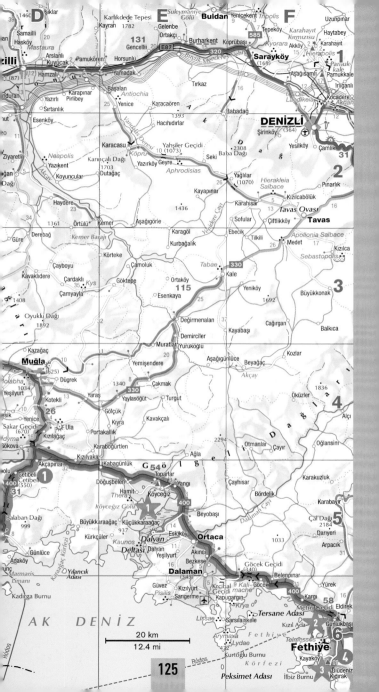

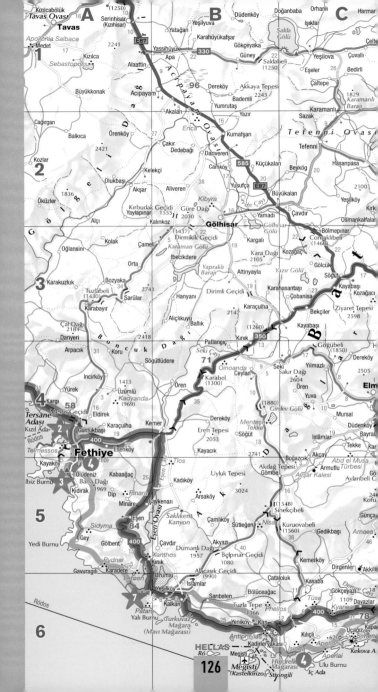

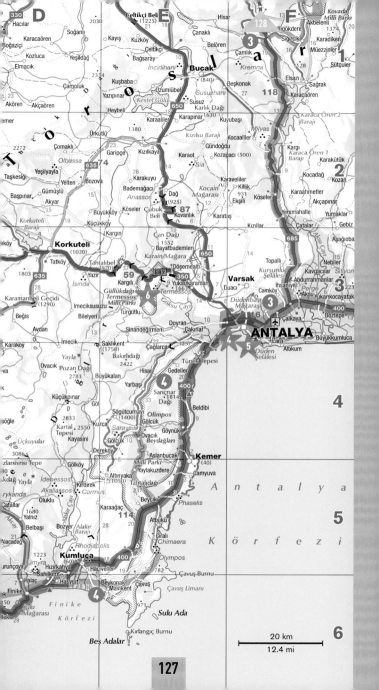

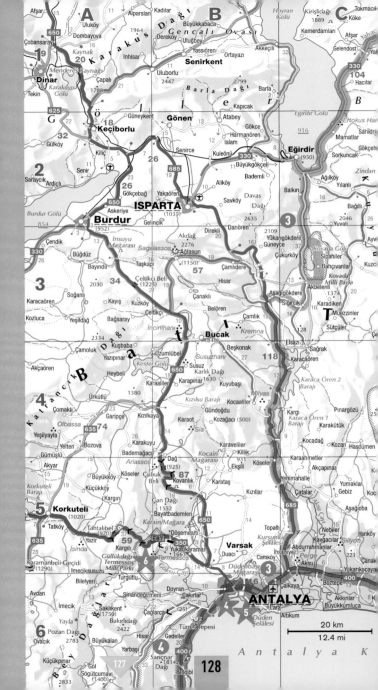

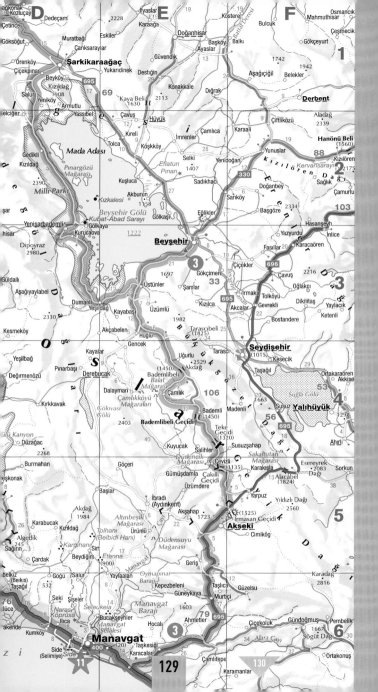

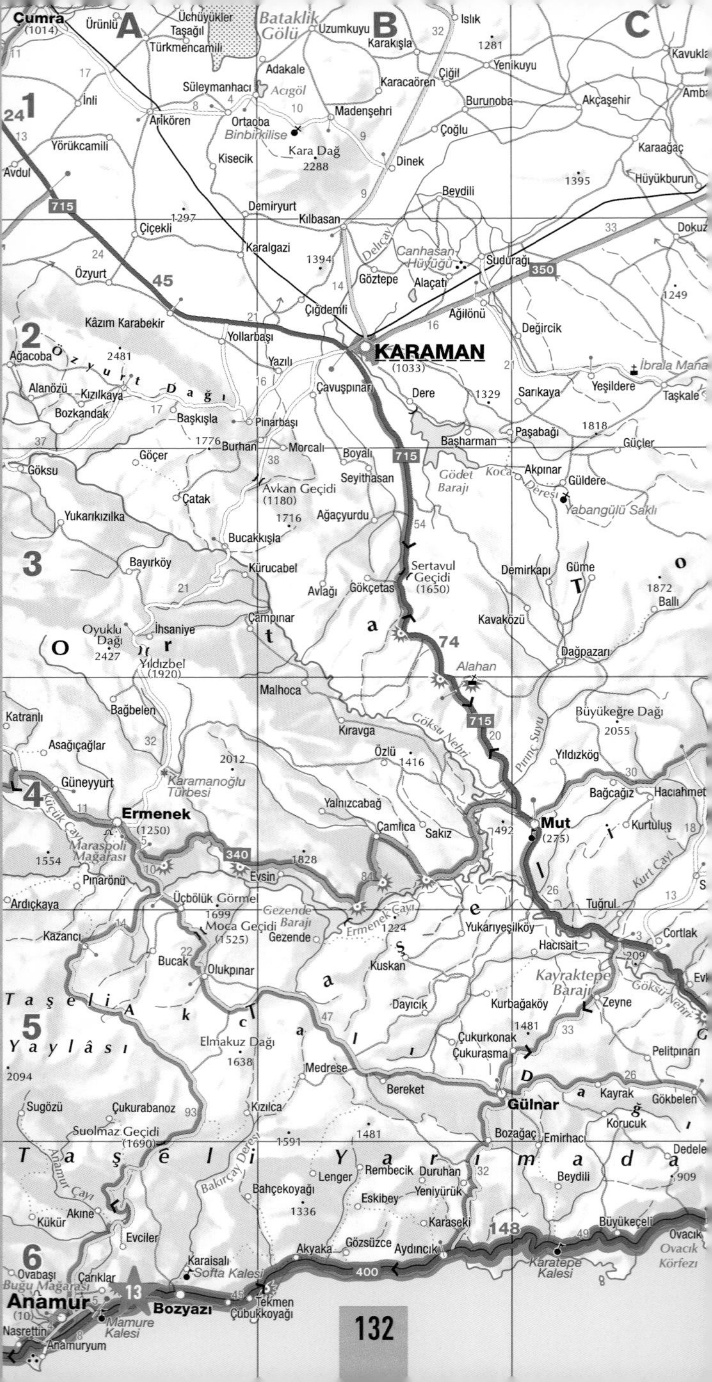
A
B
C
1
2
3
4
5
6
Çumra
(1014)
Ürünlü
Üçhüyükler
Taşağıl
Türkmencamili
Bataklık Gölü
Uzumkuyu
Karakışla
Islık
1281
Kavukla
Yenikuyu
Çiğil
Adakale
Karacaören
Süleymanhacı
Acıgöl
Burunoba
Akçaşehir
Amba
İnli
Arıkören
Ortaoba
Madenşehri
Binbirkilise
Çoğlu
Yörükcamili
Kara Dağ
2288
Kisecik
Dinek
Karaağaç
Avdul
1395
Hüyükburun
715
Beydili
Demiryurt
1297
Kılbasan
Dokuz
Çiçekli
Karalgazi
Delicay
Canhasan Hüyüğü
Sudurağı
1394
350
Özyurt
45
Göztepe
Alaçatı
1249
Ağılönü
Çiğdemli
Değircik
Kâzım Karabekir
Yollarbaşı
KARAMAN
(1033)
Ağacoba
Özyurt Dağı
2481
Yazılı
İbrala Mana
Alanözü
Kızılkaya
Çavuşpınarı
Dere
1329
Sarıkaya
Yeşildere
Taşkale
Bozkandak
Başkışla
Pınarbaşı
Paşabağı
1818
Başharman
Güçler
1776
Burhan
Morcalı
Boyalı
Göçer
38
Gödet Barajı
Koca Deresi
Akpınar
Güldere
Göksu
Seyithasan
Avkan Geçidi
(1180)
Yabangülü Saklı
Çatak
Yukarıkızılka
1716
Ağaçyurdu
54
Bucakkışla
Bayırköy
Kürücabel
Sertavul Geçidi
(1650)
Demirkapı
Güme
1872
Avlağı
Gökçetaş
Ballı
Çampınar
Kavaközü
Oyuklu Dağı
2427
İhsaniye
74
Yıldızbel
(1920)
Dağpazarı
Alahan
Malhoca
Katranlı
Bağbelen
Büyükeğre Dağı
2055
Göksu Nehri
Kıravga
Asağıçağlar
Pirinç Suyu
Özlü
1416
Yıldızköğ
2012
Güneyyurt
Karamanoğlu Türbesi
Bağcağız
Hacıahmet
Küçük Çayı
Yalnızcabağ
Ermenek
(1250)
Maraspoli Mağarası
Çamlıca
Sakız
492
Mut
(275)
Kurtuluş
340
1828
1554
Evsin
Pınarönü
Kurt Çayı
Ardıçkaya
Üçbölük
Görmel
1699
Gezende Barajı
Ermenek Çayı
Tuğrul
Moca Geçidi
(1525)
1224
Yukarıyeşilköy
Kazancı
Gezende
Hacısait
Cortlak
Bucak
Olukpınar
Kuskan
Kayraktepe Barajı
Göksu Nehri
Taşeli Yaylâsı
Akçalı Dağ
Dayıcık
Kurbağaköy
Zeyne
1481
Elmakuz Dağı
1638
Çukurkonak
Çukurasma
Pelitpınarı
2094
Medrese
Bereket
Sugözü
Çukurabanoz
Kızılca
Gülnar
Kayrak
Gökbelen
Korucuk
Suolmaz Geçidi
(1690)
1591
1481
Bozağaç
Emirhacı
Dedele
Taşeli Yarımada
Anamur Çayı
Bakırçay Deresi
Lenger
Rembecik
Duruhan
Beydili
909
Bahçekoyağı
Eskibey
Yeniyürük
Akıne
Kükür
1336
Karaseki
Büyükeçeli
148
Ovacık
Evciler
Akyaka
Gözsüzce
Aydıncık
Ovacık Körfezi
Karaisalı
Softa Kalesi
Karatepe Kalesi
400
Ovabaşı
Bugu Mağarası
Çarıklar
Anamur
(10)
13
Bozyazı
Tekmen
Çubukkoyağı
Mamure Kalesi
Nasrettin
Anamuryum

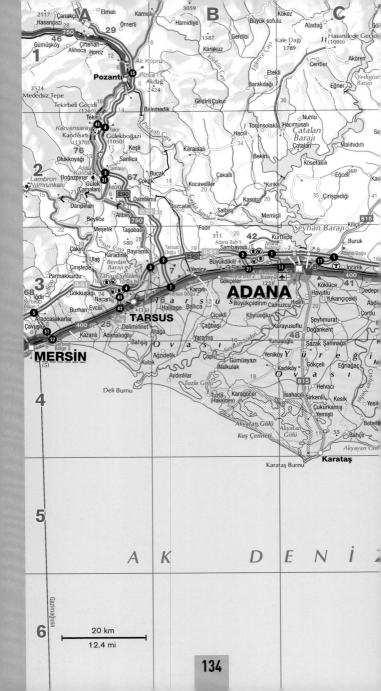

Row 1 area:
Çanakçı, Elmalı, Kamışlı, Hamidiye, Kökez, Aladağ, 3059, B, C, Hasangazi, Ömerli, Büyük sofulu, Hasandede Geçidi (1090), 2117, Gümüşköy, 750, 46, Çiftehan, Alihoca, Horoz, 29, Gerdibi, Karakuz, Kale Dağı 1789, Ceritler, Akören, Yedigöz Barajı, Ak Köprü, 1587, Etekli, Eğner, Pozantı 1 Akdağ 2424, Pozantı, 15

Row 2 area:
Mededsiz Tepe, 3524, Tekirbeli Geçidi (1260), Tekir, Belemedik, Gildirli Çukur, Nuhlu, Torunsolaklı, Hacımusalı, Çatalan Barajı, Kervansaray, Kandilsırtı (1370), Gülekboğazi (1050), Keşli, Karaisalı, Hacılı, Çatalan, Malıhıdırlı, 76, Olukkoyağı, Şanlıca, Bekirli, Kösefakılı, Lambron, Assa Kaliba, Boğazpınar, Gülek (Çamalan), Çamalan, Bucak, Çokak, Çakallı, Kocavelıler, Kırıklı, Eğceli, Namrunkale, Darıpınarı, E90, Damfama, Bozcalar, Kasoba, Çirişgediği, Beylice, Alibeyli, 750, Salbaş, Memişli, Seyhan Barajı, 815, Kilili, Meşelik, Taşobası, Fadıl, 311, Kurttepe, Buruk, Adana Doğu

Row 3 area:
Çakırlı, Bayramlı, Tarsus Çayı, 19, Adana 42, Şambayadı, Adana Kuzey1, Ulaş, Berdan Barajı, Yenice, Büyükdikilli, Adana Bab 2 Kuzey2, 11, İncirlik, Çinştepe, Parmakkurdu, Tarsus Şelalesi, Kargıli, ADANA, Köklüce, 400, 41, Gökkuşağı, Naçarlı, Ballıca, Büyükçıldırım, Camuzcu, Hıdırlı, Havutlu, Yukarıçiçekli, Dedepı, 68, İğdır, Burhan, Evcili, Halitağe, Çiçekli, Köylüoğlu, Karayusuflu, Şeyhmurat, Doğankent, Çortlu, Arapçasakarlar, TARSUS, Deliminnet, Allağa, Çağbaşı, Abdı, Çavuşlu, Kazanlı, Adanalıoğlu, Bahşiş, Yaramış, Yunusoğlu, Sazak Şahinağa

Row 4 area:
MERSİN, Kulak, Ağızdelik, Çöplü, Gümüsyazı, Nalkulak, Yeniköy, Kadıköy, Gökçeli, Eğriağaç, Deli Burnu, Aydınlılar, Tuzla Gölü, Tuzla (Hakkibey), Karagöçer, İsahacılı, Helvacı, Sirkenli, Kesik, Yesil, Akyatan Gölü, Akyatan Gölü, Çukurkamış, Yemişli, Bebel, Kuş Çenneti, Bahçe, Akyayan Göl, Karataş Burnu, Karataş

Row 5–6 area:
A K D E N İ Z

20 km
12.4 mi

134

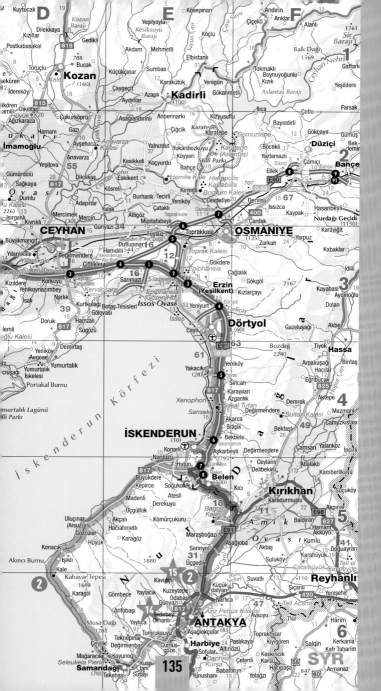

KEY TO ROAD ATLAS

🔴18 🔴26 ● Motorway with junctions
Autobahn mit Anschlussstellen

Motorway under construction
Autobahn in Bau

▮ Toll station
Mautstelle

🅾 Roadside restaurant and hotel
Raststätte mit Übernachtung

🄋 Roadside restaurant
Raststätte

🄌 Filling-station
Tankstelle

Dual carriage-way with
motorway characteristics
with junction
Autobahnähnliche Schnell-
straße mit Anschlussstelle

Trunk road
Fernverkehrsstraße

Thoroughfare
Durchgangsstraße

Important main road
Wichtige Hauptstraße

Main road
Hauptstraße

Secondary road
Nebenstraße

Railway
Eisenbahn

🚗 Car-loading terminal
Autozug-Terminal

Mountain railway
Zahnradbahn

Aerial cableway
Kabinenschwebebahn

Railway ferry
Eisenbahnfähre

🚢 Car ferry
Autofähre

Shipping route
Schifffahrtslinie

Route with
beautiful scenery
Landschaftlich besonders
schöne Strecke

Alleenstr. Tourist route
Touristenstraße

XI-V Closure in winter
Wintersperre

×××× Road closed to motor traffic
Straße für Kfz gesperrt

8% Important gradients
Bedeutende Steigungen

🚐 Not recommended
for caravans
Für Wohnwagen nicht
empfehlenswert

🚐 Closed for caravans
Für Wohnwagen gesperrt

☀ Important panoramic view
Besonders schöner Ausblick

✳ *Wartenstein* Of interest: culture - nature
✳ *Umbalfälle* Sehenswert: Kultur - Natur

Bathing beach
Badestrand

National park, nature park
Nationalpark, Naturpark

Prohibited area
Sperrgebiet

⌓ Church
Kirche

⌓ Monastery
Kloster

⌓ Palace, castle
Schloss, Burg

⌓ Mosque
Moschee

⌓ ⌓ ⌓ ⌓ Ruins
Ruinen

⌓ Lighthouse
Leuchtturm

⌓ Tower
Turm

∩ Cave
Höhle

∴ Archaeological excavation
Ausgrabungsstätte

▲ Youth hostel
Jugendherberge

🏠 Isolated hotel
Allein stehendes Hotel

🏠 Refuge
Berghütte

▲ Camping site
Campingplatz

✈ Airport
Flughafen

✈ Regional airport
Regionalflughafen

✈ Airfield
Flugplatz

National boundary
Staatsgrenze

Administrative boundary
Verwaltungsgrenze

⊖ Check-point
Grenzkontrollstelle

⊖ Check-point with
restrictions
Grenzkontrollstelle mit
Beschränkung

ROMA Capital
Hauptstadt

VENÉZIA Seat of the administration
Verwaltungssitz

Trips & tours
Ausflüge & Touren

Perfect route
Perfekte Route

⭐1 MARCO POLO Highlight

INDEX

This index lists all places and sights, plus the names of important people and key words featured in this guide. Numbers in bold indicate a main entry.

CREDITS

WRITE TO US

e-mail: info@marcopologuides.co.uk

Did you have a great holiday? Is there something on your mind? Whatever it is, let us know! Whether you want to praise, alert us to errors or give us a personal tip – MARCO POLO would be pleased to hear from you. We do everything we can to provide the very latest information for your trip.

Nevertheless, despite all of our authors' thorough research, errors can creep in. MARCO POLO does not accept any liability for this. Please contact us by e-mail or post.

MARCO POLO Travel Publishing Ltd Pinewood, Chineham Business Park Crockford Lane, Chineham Basingstoke, Hampshire RG24 8AL United Kingdom

PICTURE CREDITS
Cover photograph: Kaleköy harbour (Look/SagaPhoto: Forget)
Özlem Ahmetoğlu (17 bottom); DuMont Bildarchiv: Spitta (40/41, 85, 106/107), Wrba (front flap right, 47, 49, 62, 94, 104); ©fotolia.com: aktifreklam (16 top), Ann Thibeault (16 bottom); J. Gottschlich/D. Zaptçioğlu (1 bottom); R. Hackenberg (2 centre top, 2 bottom, 7, 8, 20, 30 right, 39, 50/51, 59, 65, 69, 72, 76, 77, 87, 88, 91, 106, 107, 122/123); Hip-Notics Cable Park: Barış Özoral (17 top); Huber: Schmid (front flap left, 3 bottom, 10/11, 92/93, 137); M. Kirchgessner (18/19); Laif: Glaescher (102/103), hemis (108 top), Tophoven (27), Tueremis (2 centre bottom, 24/25, 32/33); Laif/Nar Photos: Stringe (3 centre, 80/81); Look/SagaPhoto: Forget (1 top, 114); mauritius images: Alamy (2 top, 4, 5, 9, 12/13, 26 right, 28/29, 30 left, 37, 42, 55, 56, 66, 82, 98/99, 100, 105, 108 bottom, 109), Hänel (79), Hubatka (3top, 70/71), World Pictures (75); Mavi Jeans (16 centre); R. Renckhoff (26 left); Visum: Reents (28); E. Wrba (6, 15, 22, 29, 44, 52, 58, 61, 96); M. Zegers (34)

1st Edition 2012
Worldwide Distribution: Marco Polo Travel Publishing Ltd, Pinewood, Chineham Business Park, Crockford Lane, Basingstoke, Hampshire RG24 8AL, United Kingdom. Email: sales@marcopolouk.com
© MAIRDUMONT GmbH & Co. KG, Ostfildern
Chief editors: Michaela Lienemann (concept, managing editor), Marion Zorn (concept, text editor)
Author: Dilek Zaptçioğlu, Jürgen Gottschlich; editor: Jochen Schürmann
Programme supervision: Ann-Katrin Kutzner, Nikolai Michaelis, Silwen Randebrock
Picture editor: Gabriele Forst
What's hot: wunder media, Munich
Cartography road atlas: © MAIRDUMONT, Ostfildern; Cartography pull-out map: © MAIRDUMONT, Ostfildern
Design: milchhof: atelier, Berlin; Front cover, pull-out map cover, page 1: factor product munich
Translated from German by Robert Scott McInnes; editor of the English edition: Christopher Wynne
Prepress: M. Feuerstein, Wigel
Phrase book in cooperation with Ernst Klett Sprachen GmbH, Stuttgart, Editorial by Pons Wörterbücher

DOS & DON'TS 👆

A few tips to help you avoid having problems in Turkey

DON'T BECOME A VICTIM OF RIP-OFF ARTISTS & TOUTS

They always show up where there a lot of tourists; the seemingly friendly locals who know where you can buy the cheapest carpets and eat at the best restaurants. They are usually touts who get a commission for bringing clients to shops and hotels. The rip-off artists are another matter; they invite tourists to have a drink, take them to dubious establishments and then present them with an astronomical bill. Be careful about letting people invite you to a nightclub or disco – it can end up being a very expensive evening!

BE CAREFUL ABOUT WHAT YOU DRINK

There have been several cases of serious alcohol poisoning in Turkey and, on no account, should you be tempted to buy cheap spirits in small shops. The illegally distilled booze contains methyl alcohol and can be lethal. Buy your drinks in supermarkets or in so-called *Tekel* shops where you see a lot of customers. If you feel ill, call an ambulance (112) immediately or take a taxi to the nearest hospital *(hastane)*.

DON'T DISCUSS POLITICS WITH STRANGERS

There is no way to be sure that your Turkish vis-à-vis shares your opinions about religion, the founder of the state or its minority groups. Rashly begun discussions can rapidly lead to frustra-

tions for all involved. Many Turks are no longer as positive about the EU as they were only a short time ago. It is a better idea to talk about the weather if you don't know the person well.

MAKE SURE YOUR CLOTHING IS NOT TOO CASUAL

Wearing a swimsuit in a restaurant or shorts in a mosque will not only meet with disapprovement, it is usually not allowed. Restaurants on beaches also expect their guests to observe a minimum of decorum and you only enter houses of worship – regardless of whether it is a church, synagogue or mosque – decently dressed. And, don't forget to take off your shoes before you go into a mosque.

NUDE BATHING

Topless bathing is quite common at many resorts. But you should be a little more prudent on public beaches where you will be met with disapproving looks. Nude bathing not only does not go down well in Turkey – it is forbidden.

SMOOCHING IN PUBLIC

It might be fairly common in Marmaris, but in Konya in Central Anatolia it could be a problem. Showing affection in public – such as kissing going beyond the standard welcoming peck – is not actually forbidden but should respect the customs of the host country.